REFEREE

12th Edition

HIGH SCHOOL FOOTBALL

PENALTY ENFORCEMENTS MADE EASY

By Jeffrey Stern

On the Cover

Sterling K. del Rey, Las Vegas, began officiating football in 2010. He has worked youth leagues, middle through high school, to men's league games. He aspires to work higher level college games in the future.
Photo: Dale Garvey

High School Football Penalty Enforcements Made Easy – *12th Edition*

By Jeffrey Stern, senior editor, *Referee* magazine

Published by Referee Enterprises, Inc. (www.referee.com)
and the National Association of Sports Officials (www.naso.org)

Printed in the United States of America

ISBN-13: 978-1-58208-527-2

TABLE OF CONTENTS

TABLE OF CONTENTS

INTRODUCTION

Calling a foul and enforcing a penalty aren't as easy as coaches and fans think it is. It takes solid rules knowledge, great judgment, communication and complete knowledge of the mechanics involved.

This book won't magically give you better judgment, but it will help you understand the hows and whys of the process, from the time the flag is thrown until the ball is next snapped or kicked.

When a crew messes up any part of a penalty enforcement, the entire crew is to blame. That's why *High School Penalty Enforcements Made Easy* isn't written from an individual perspective. Every official should — make that must — know the procedures.

The first five chapters take you through the process. Chapters 6 through 17 explain the various types of plays on which fouls occur and how they are handled. They are broken up into categories. The idea to place penalty enforcements into slots sprang from the mind of Tom Kelleher, an NFL official from 1960-87. Ed Hochuli, one of the best referees to ever work in the NFL, has refined it. Karl Richins, former collegiate referee and current coordinator of officials for the Big Sky Conference, adapted Hochuli's idea into one for college rules. Richins shared it with *Referee*, a partnership was born and we decided high school officials would benefit from one too.

This book is designed to simplify how penalties are enforced. It is a reference and study tool to help you make penalty enforcement second nature.

Here's hoping you find this book as helpful as I have.

Jeffrey Stern
Senior editor
Referee magazine

CHAPTER 1

CALLING A FOUL AND USING THE FLAG

PlayPic®

When you observe a live-ball foul, it is crucial that you drop your penalty marker at the proper yardline but withhold the whistle until the play is over. Make a mental note of the spot of the foul and the number of the offending player but continue to officiate the play; don't stop at the spot of the foul and fail to cover the play to its conclusion.

If the spot of the foul will be the enforcement spot, you must get your flag as close to that spot as possible. If you're off target, you should relocate the flag as soon as possible after the play by picking it up and moving it definitively. The longer you delay making that correction, the more it will appear you are manipulating the situation. Also, attempting to kick it to the correct spot gives an underhanded appearance.

Correct penalty enforcement can be facilitated if the flag is thrown properly. There are two ways to throw the flag: into the air or carefully to a spot.

Throw the flag at the spot, not the players.

In PlayPic A, the referee sees a live-ball foul: the offensive lineman holding the pass rusher. Because the penalty may be enforced from the spot of the foul, it is important for the referee to throw his flag to the yardline on which the infraction was committed. The flag should be thrown so that it hits the ground on either side of the players;

don't think of the player as a dart board and your flag as a dart. Throwing the flag in the direction of the players will help the referee observe the number of the offending player. Whether an overhand or underhand motion is used is up to the individual.

For dead-ball fouls or fouls simultaneous with the snap, such as a false start or encroachment, the whistle should be blown immediately and the flag should be tossed into the air directly in front of you. In PlayPic B, a defensive player has committed a dead-ball foul by crossing the neutral zone and contacting a team A player. The flag should be thrown into the air in front of you and the stop-the-clock signal given. Again, don't stop officiating. The offensive lineman could take exception to the penalty and retaliate. Once you are confident the action has stopped, jog toward the center of the field and report the foul to the referee. Don't signal; the other wing official may well have a different view or another foul.

For fouls that prevent the snap, throw the flag into the air.

It is strongly recommended that an official who throws a flag or sees one on the field use three short blasts on the whistle after the ball is dead to bring the flag to the referee's attention. The whistle should be accompanied by the stop-the-clock signal.

Sometimes the calling official has to leave the spot of the flag to report to the referee. If feasible, another official should stand at the spot to ensure the flag isn't moved.

If two different officials throw flags on the same play, it is important they communicate to see if they saw the same foul or have two different fouls.

A few techniques to avoid: slam-dunking the flag to the ground; looking angry when you toss it; holding the flag and waving it, instead of throwing it; or throwing it at the fouling player. On late hits, the latter looks confrontational, and worse yet, might hit the player in the face.

ME-TOO FLAGS

Avoid throwing "me-too" flags. That involves having the official closest to the official who threw his flag also throwing his flag as a means of supporting his partner. The concept is the coach will think it is an acceptable call because two officials had it. The technique is both unnecessary and deceptive.

While there are some situations in which the coverage will overlap two officials, many plays dictate each official maintain unique coverage. Further, if the two officials were to offer contradicting explanations of the foul, the crew's integrity would be severely diminished. Finally, excessive flags will contribute to an image of a "flag happy" crew.

CHAPTER 2

REPORTING A FOUL

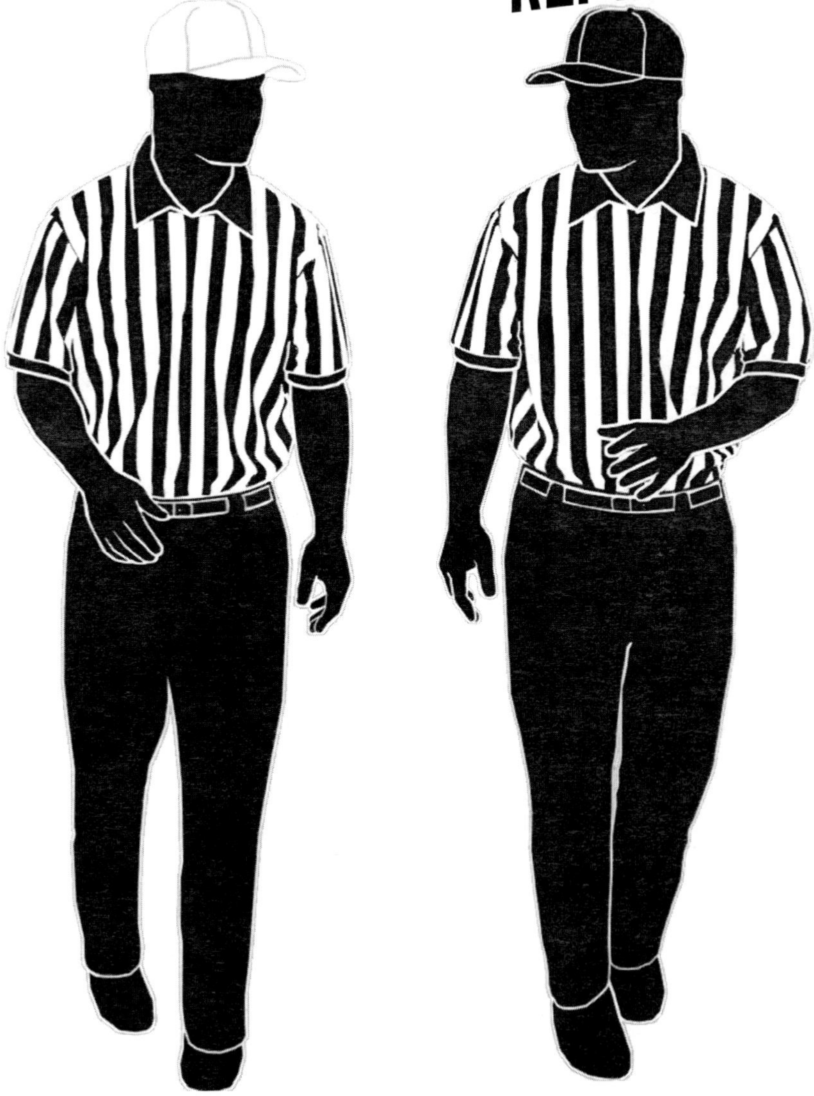

Fouls must be reported to the press box and both coaches. Additionally, all fouls must be communicated to all members of the officiating crew as each official has a role in penalty enforcement.

Once the flag is thrown, the official who threw it must ensure both the referee and linesman are aware as soon as possible after the play ends. The linesman will ensure the chains and box are not moved and the referee will prepare for the steps that follow.

The referee's first step in quality communication is to get an accurate report from the official who threw the flag. The referee must then move clear of the players, face the press box, stand stationary and indicate the foul and the offending team using the appropriate signal.

Do not signal fouls from your position.

When wing officials throw a flag for a dead-ball foul prior to the snap, they should jog slowly toward the middle of the field to report the foul to the referee. Remember to practice good dead-ball officiating during the jog; if a player has crossed the neutral zone and contacted an opponent, the contacted opponent may try to retaliate.

A technique to avoid is signaling the foul rather

than reporting the foul to the referee (PlayPic C). It's common in the NFL and major college games, but should not be practiced at other levels because another official may have a different foul. For instance, say the line judge throws a flag because a team B player entered the neutral zone and contacted the left guard but the umpire throws a flag because the snapper illegally moved the ball. If the line judge stays on the wing, gives the hands-on-hips signal and points to the defense but the penalty is assessed against the offense, the coach of the offensive team is certain to be upset. Instead of signaling from the wing, in that case the linesman, line judge and umpire should get together to discuss what each official has seen, then report their decision to the referee. The wing officials then return to the sidelines to explain to the coaches what occurred.

Keep your hands off each other when discussing a play.

Conferences among officials should be kept as brief as possible. When reporting a foul, be thorough but give the referee only the information he needs.

If two or more officials need to discuss a call, avoid putting arms around another official's waist or back (PlayPic D, page 14). It gives the appearance the officials are conspiring or are trying to convince another official what he should be calling.

GETTING THE EXPLANATION

Some referees simply want to hear the foul and offender, such as, "No. 49 offense, illegal motion." Other referees prefer to be told what the reporting official saw, as in, "No. 49 cut upfield too soon." It may make sense to use both techniques depending on the experience level of the crewmate. By getting more detail from newer officials, the referee can ensure there really was a foul. Be careful with movement fouls when the order of occurrence is a prime factor and be especially careful if offensive players on the end of line are involved — their movement is not as restricted as it is for the interior linemen who cannot move from a three-point stance.

On certain fouls, it is critical that the referee be told the status of the ball when the foul occurred or whether a player involved was an eligible receiver. Of course the guilty team must also be identified. The trend at many levels is to get away from referring to teams by jersey color. The pregame conference should include a discussion of how to report fouls.

GIVING THE EXPLANATION

When it is obvious to the referee that a penalty will be accepted, the captain need not be consulted. A good example involves a team A foul that occurs prior to a turnover. Team B will obviously want to decline the penalty and take possession. If a choice needs to be made, all aspects of the penalty (e.g. an automatic first down, ejection, etc.) should be explained to the captain. State the options briefly, but correctly, clearly and courteously. The umpire must listen to the referee's explanation to ensure the options are properly offered.

The wing official on the sideline of the penalized team should tell the coach the number of the guilty player and explain the foul. The call gains credibility if you say, "Your man in motion cut upfield too soon," instead of, "There was illegal motion." The other wing official need only tell the coach the nature of the foul.

Once the referee determines whether the penalty has been accepted or declined, he must inform other members of the crew. If the penalty is accepted, the umpire must understand where to walk from – the enforcement spot, how far to walk and which direction to walk. It's quite embarrassing to have the penalty enforced against the offended team and having to reverse tracks amid the inevitable protests.

The wing officials must be apprised so they can keep their sideline informed. The wing on the offending team's sideline should tell the coach the number of the player who fouled; however, if the covering official didn't get the number, he shouldn't guess or make one up. If a non-existent number is reported, crew credibility is immediately destroyed.

WORKING WITH CAPTAINS AND COACHES

When the referee and umpire meet with the coaches prior to the game, they should obtain the name and number of each captain. Communication between officials and captains can affect the flow of the game. Knowing when and in what depth to talk to captains can avoid unnecessary delay.

There are situations in which it is more realistic to consult the coach rather than the captain. For example: Team K punts on fourth and seven from its own 35 yardline. Team R is flagged for running into the kicker, which carries a five-yard penalty. Team R makes a fair catch at its own 40 yardline. Team K's coach may wish to accept the penalty, bringing up fourth and two, and go for the first down, or decline the penalty because he is happy with team R's field position. Ultimately (and realistically) the coach will make the decision anyway. Rather than explaining the options to the captain, the wing official on that side of the field should explain the options to the coach and relay the decision to the referee.

A similar situation occurs when team K's free kick goes out of bounds untouched by team R. Team R has the choice of a rekick after enforcement, taking the ball 25 yards from the spot of the kick or taking a five-yard penalty from the spot the ball went out of bounds. Rather than have the referee (who begins the play at team R's goalline), sprint upfield and try to find a captain, the official on team R's side of the field and nearest to team R's coach can explain the options.

CHAPTER 2

A foul by the defense on a try will move the ball to the 1-1/2 yardline. If team A is not considering going for two points, it may very well want to decline the penalty, stick to its normal routine and kick from the spot it has practiced a thousand times.

When the offense chooses to punt because it is just out of field goal range, teams will often intentionally incur a penalty for delay. The strategy is to have five more yards to put the punt out of bounds deeper in the opponent's territory and avoid the touchback. Team B may prefer to decline the penalty and foil the strategy.

That situation brings into focus another time the crew will have to work with the coaches and each other. When a penalty is accepted with less than two minutes remaining in either half, the offended team will have the option to start the game clock on the snap.

The wing official on the offended team's sideline should find out if the coach wishes to exercise the clock-on-the-snap option. If so, the opposite wing informs the coach of the offending team.

Conversely, if the option is not exercised by the coach of the offended team and the clock is to start on the ready, the offending team may use a charged team timeout (if the team has one remaining) to keep the clock from starting until the next snap.

Those are classic examples of why it is important for every official to know and understand penalties and enforcements.

REPORTING A FOUL

There are several types of fouls that will always be accepted, thus consultation with the captain is unnecessary:

• **Dead-ball fouls.** Since the replay of a down is not in question, the distance is gratis. Remember, however, that some dead-ball fouls that occur after a score may be enforced on the succeeding kickoff. Penalties for unsportsmanlike conduct are enforced as if they are dead-ball fouls and will likely be accepted.

• **Fouls after a change of possession.** Certain fouls during kickoff, punt, interception and fumble returns are similar to dead-ball fouls in that there is no down to replay. The interests of the game are best served by immediately walking off those penalties. If there is more than one foul against the same team, you can easily figure out which penalty will yield the greatest benefit.

• **Fouls that negate scores, turnovers and first downs.**

• **"Add on" or "tack-on" fouls.** Examples of live-ball fouls that add yardage to the end of a play include a defensive facemask foul on a running play and roughing the passer on a completed pass.

• **Loss of down/automatic first down.** It would be most unusual for a team not to want a penalty that carries loss of down or an automatic first down.

Declination of a penalty can also be an obvious choice. When a play results in a first down and the penalty would not, you can signal the refusal without discussion.

CHAPTER 3

ENFORCING THE PENALTY

If the penalty has previous-spot enforcement, the umpire must return not only to the yardline at which the ball was last snapped, he must also go back to the spot between the hashes (the lateral position of the ball).

In MechaniGram E, team A is snapping from the hashmark on its own 20 yardline. In MechaniGram F, A2 is flagged for illegal motion as A1 completes a pass to A3 closer to the opposite hash. A3 is immediately tackled by B4.

When team B accepts the penalty, the umpire must return to the exact place from which the play started — that is, the same hashmark on team A's 20 yardline — and the penalty is enforced from there (MechaniGram G).

The umpire should avoid "marching off the penalty" a yard at a time. It looks far more professional to calculate the distance from the enforcement spot and go directly to the proper yardline. For instance: Team A is to

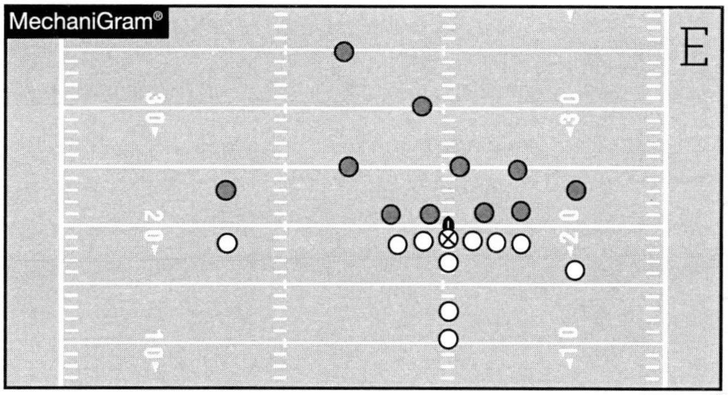

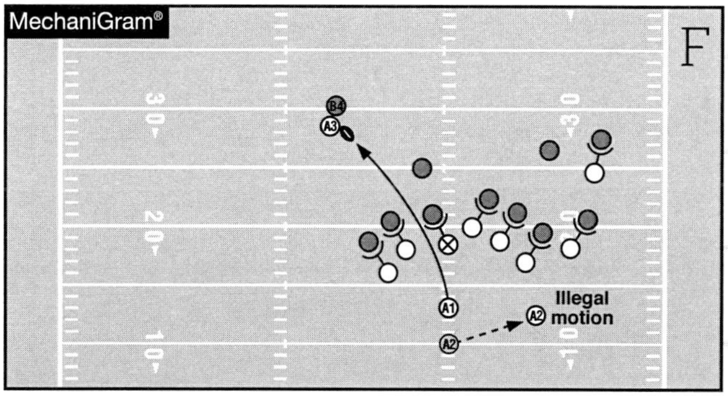

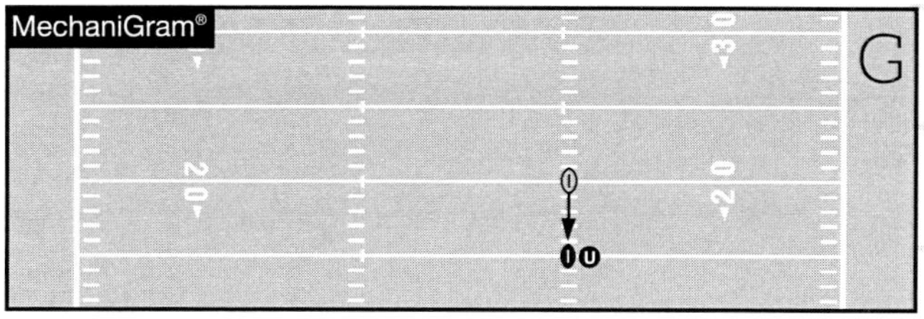

be penalized for holding. The spot of enforcement is team A's 37 yardline. The umpire should move briskly and directly to team A's 27 yardline and place the ball.

The linesman must be certain of the down number. Don't forget that acceptance of a penalty that includes loss of down or declination of a penalty will not result in a replay of the previous down.

As a backup to ensure the umpire has properly enforced the penalty, the linesman should proceed to the succeeding spot. Once the penalty is enforced, the linesman should have the down box, the line-to-gain equipment or both moved.

The linesman goes to the succeeding spot as the referee signals.

As seen in PlayPic H, the line judge has flagged team A for a five-yard, dead-ball foul. As the referee is signaling the foul, the linesman moves to the succeeding spot. The umpire should still calculate where the ball should be placed and take it to that spot, but if the penalty is enforced correctly, that spot will be where the linesman has already placed himself.

In order to use the mechanic properly, the linesman must obtain the penalty information from the referee and umpire. The linesman can then report the foul to the head coach on his side of the field before moving to the succeeding spot. In the pregame meeting with the chain crew, the linesman must emphasize that the chains should not be moved until the linesman signals them to do so. That prevents a premature or incorrect movement of the box and chains. The line judge should stand at the enforcement spot until the ball is marked ready for play.

Notice the line judge has not moved off the previous line of scrimmage. That is a good back up in case the chains move incorrectly or prematurely.

From the time the whistle blows to prevent the snap or indicate the ball is dead until the referee next signals the ball is ready, any official not involved in the enforcement process must watch the players. If players from both teams are congregating, the back judge in a crew of five may have to move up toward the line to let players know they should return to their respective sides of the ball.

Finally, the referee should again move clear of the players, face the press box, stand stationary and indicate the foul and the offending team using the appropriate signals.

Many fouls, such as false start, delay of game and encroachment, are self-evident to players, coaches, fans and public address announcers. Those fouls do not require a preliminary signal and then another signal after enforcement.

Just as officials should avoid making calls on the

run, referees should avoid "walking through" their penalty signals. Walking through means failing to come to a complete stop before signaling, as seen in PlayPic I.

Referees should avoid "walking through" their signals.

To give the signal to the press box, keep your head up. Pick out a spot about halfway up the stands and focus your eyes on that spot. You should have no facial expression; you're neither happy nor unhappy to be performing the task.

Give the signal and point to the offending team. Avoid jabbing the arm when signaling; it is another sign you are angry or feel a sense of "gotcha" toward the offending team.

Referees should avoid the habit of striving to get between the hashes to signal every penalty. If a play ends in a side zone, you only need to be clear of players in order to signal a penalty.

Remind the referee to start the clock on the ready (left) or snap.

Once the referee ensures all officials, the box and chains are in their proper places, he can give the ready signal.

ENFORCING THE PENALTY

The referee has a lot on his mind when enforcing a penalty. The line judge can help by reminding the referee when the clock should start. After the referee has signaled the press box, he need only glance at the line judge to see if the wing official is rotating his index finger (PlayPic J, page 24), which indicates the clock starts on the ready, or snapping his fingers (PlayPic K, page 24), which indicates the clock starts on the snap. Many crews have adopted other signals; the important thing is that the information is conveyed. It is suggested that the line judge perform that duty since the referee is already facing the line judge to signal the press box.

UNSPORTSMANLIKE FOULS AND EJECTIONS

For all unsportsmanlike fouls, all officials should record the player's number or the coach's position (i.e. head coach, offensive coordinator, etc.). Remember that a second unsportsmanlike foul against the same individual results in his ejection, but a flagrant foul (personal or unsportsmanlike) results in immediate ejection.

Only the referee should use the ejection signal, and only when signaling the penalty to the press box. Use the approved signal, not a baseball-style windup and throw.

If the penalty for a foul includes ejecting the offender, the official who called the foul must inform the offending player. The official should report the player's number and the type of infraction to referee, coach and other members of the officiating crew. Keep in mind the coach will likely want a more detailed description than of a more routine foul.

CHAPTER 3

All officials should record the ejected player's number and the time of the ejection. The calling official may want to write a brief description of the incident on his game card or a separate card in order to properly report the incident to the state association or similar authority.

Remember that if a coach is ejected, he must leave the stadium area before the game may resume and the coach may not have further contact with his team for the remainder of the game including halftime. Ejected players are not required to leave the field.

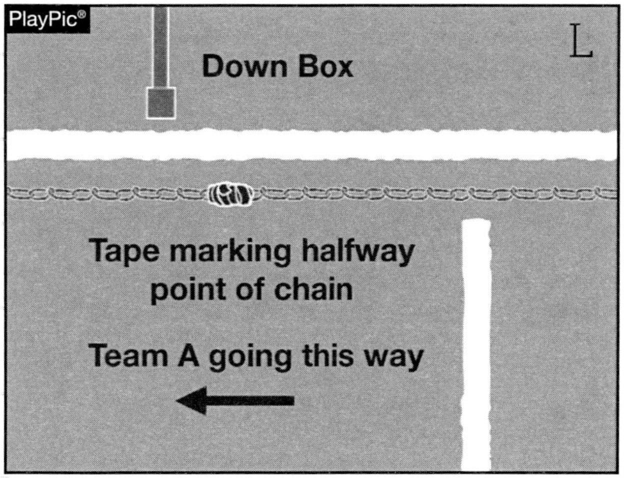

Tape on the chain helps determine if team A has less than five yards for a first down.

The linesman indicating "five will get you one."

HELPING THE REFEREE

Crews can expedite penalty enforcement and avoid unnecessary measurements through communication between the referee and linesman.

In PlayPic L, the down box is farther downfield than the

tape used to indicate the halfway point on the chain. That means a five-yard penalty on team B will result in a first down for team A, or as often abbreviated by crews, "Five will get you one."

The linesman can indicate the situation by making eye contact with the referee and placing the palm of his hand flat against his chest (PlayPic M, page 26). If a team B foul such as encroachment occurs, the referee already knows that a new series will be awarded.

NOTE: The chain and box are not shown in the proper place two yards outside the sideline in order to better illustrate the point.

One of the hazards of being a wing official is being the target of angry coaches, even when the wing official hasn't made the call in question. Brisk and businesslike penalty administration will get the ball in play more quickly, thus diverting the attention of the angry coaches. If the referee has made the call, the wing official can help the referee simply by standing near the flag.

In PlayPic N (on page 28), the quarterback, having been flushed from the pocket by a hard-charging defender, was roughed after releasing the pass. The referee has properly followed the flow of the play toward team B's sideline and is in position to flag the foul while the wing official is observing players downfield.

Because the foul occurred in front of team B's bench, the sideline may well erupt in anger. It is tempting for the referee to remain in front of the bench and argue or try to explain the call. A better procedure is for the wing official (in this case, the linesman) to come back to the spot of the flag and mark the spot while the referee gives the preliminary signal (PlayPic O) and works with the umpire to enforce the penalty.

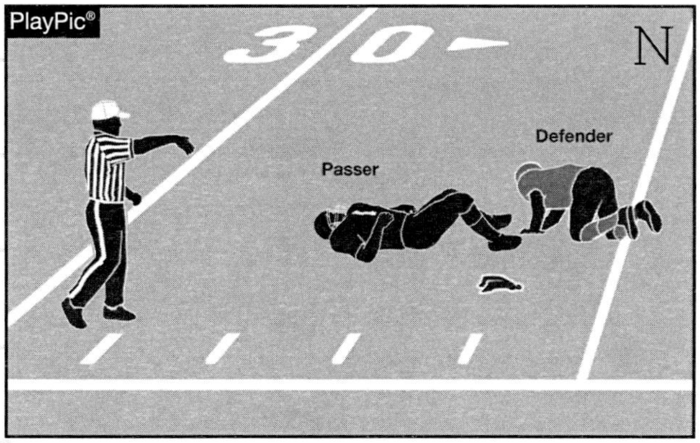

If the referee has a foul near the fouling team's sideline (above), the wing official can stand over the flag while the referee can move farther away from any angry coaches.

The wing official on the opposite side of the field (in this case, the line judge) should casually walk off the penalty to serve as a backup for the umpire. The umpire and line judge should wind up at the same spot; if not, the proper spot should be determined before the umpire places the ball on the ground and the chains set at the new spot. If done properly, the line judge will be mirroring the umpire's spot.

Once the penalty has been enforced and the ball properly spotted, the linesman should pick up the flag, jog to the middle of the field and toss or hand the flag back to the referee (PlayPic P, page 29).

'EATING' A FLAG

Every official has made a call he would like to have back. Thus, the timeless advice, "When in doubt, don't throw the flag," or, "If you see a foul, flag it, but if you only think it's a foul, don't."

In addition to officials occasionally asking each other for help, a "change of heart" flag can occur once in a while as well. Although those are difficult to explain to coaches, it's unfair to penalize a team when the covering official suddenly realizes he isn't sure a foul occurred.

If you feel you've thrown an erroneous flag, explain the situation to the referee. Both coaches will want to know what's going on. But only the referee should "wave off the flag" as seen in PlayPic Q.

By returning the flag to the referee in the middle of the field, the wing official can keep the referee away from the sideline.

Only the referee should give the signal for ignoring the flag.

CHAPTER 4

PENALTY SIGNALING SEQUENCES

PlayPic®

The order of the penalty signals used by the referee is just as important as the clarity of the signals. Think of signal sequence as words in a sentence. The singular words, "Sequence important the is the of signals," makes little sense when thought of as individual words. But "The sequence of the signals is important," uses the same words and is easy to understand.

The key to quality signaling is remembering that it is a sequence of fluid movements. Take your time. Signals executed with separate and distinct motions ensure clarity; jumbled quickly together and the messages are lost. Also, remember to wait for the linesman to indicate the chains are in position and the rest of the crew is in place before giving the ready-for-play.

It is also important to face the proper direction when giving the signal. All signals are given facing the press box.

The ready-for-play signal can be the downward stroke of your arm for the start-the-clock signal when the clock starts on the ready.

SIGNALING LIVE-BALL FOULS

Signaling the penalty for a run-of-the-mill live-ball foul is a four-step process: foul signal, a point toward the team that fouled, an indication of the next down and either the ready-for-play or start-the-clock signal. Other signals, such as loss of down or an ejection signal, may need to be added. But in most cases, only four signals are needed.

One example of a typical penalty signaling sequence involves roughing the passer. As seen in

CHAPTER 4

PlayPic R, the referee signals the foul (1), indicates which team has fouled (2) and signals that team A has been awarded a new series (3). The referee waits to be sure the chains have been moved and the other officials are in position. If the pass was complete and the runner was downed inbounds, the referee blows his whistle and simultaneously gives the start-the-clock signal (4). If the pass was incomplete or the play ended out of bounds, the referee gives the ready-for-play while simultaneously blowing his whistle (5).

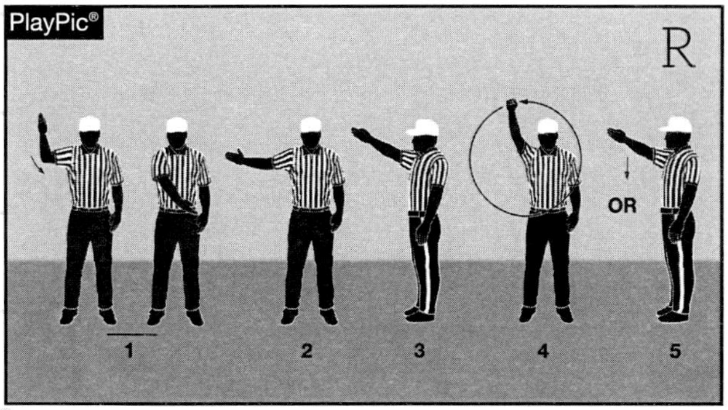

Say team B has been called for roughing the passer but team A scored a touchdown. The scoring team may choose to have the penalty enforced on the try. If so, the sequence in PlayPic S is used with the ready signal. If the scoring team chooses to have the penalty enforced on the next kickoff, the referee signals the foul (1) and indicates which team has fouled (2). The referee signals the touchdown (3), then points to the spot of the next kickoff to indicate the enforcement (4).

In PlayPic T on page 33, the defense has been called for holding. The referee first indicates the foul (1), followed by the fouling team (2). If the penalty results in a first down, the referee signals that team A has been awarded a new series (3). If the runner was downed inbounds, the referee blows his whistle and simultaneously gives the start-the-clock signal (4). For an incomplete pass or if the play ended out of bounds, the referee gives the ready-for-play while simultaneously blowing his whistle (5).

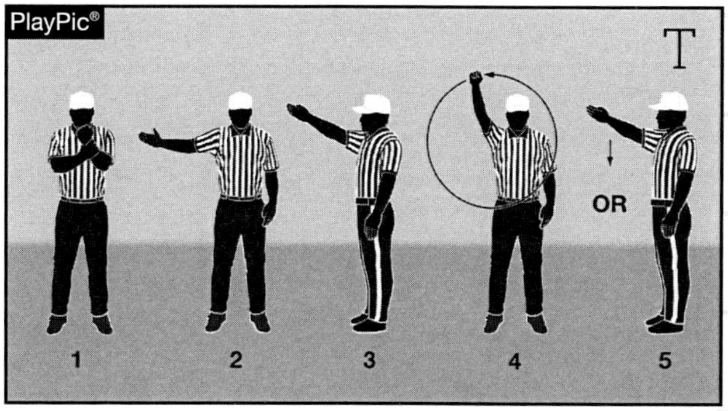

Cases that involve an ejection add a step to the process. The referee must indicate the decision to the press box. PlayPic U illustrates the sequence for a live-ball foul for illegal helmet contact that results in an ejection. The referee first indicates the nature of the foul (1) and the fouling team (2). The ejection is then indicated (3). If the penalty results in a first down, the referee signals that team A has been awarded a new series (4); if not, the referee signals the next down. In this example, the penalty has given team A sufficient yardage for a first down. If the previous play ended inbounds, the referee blows his whistle and simultaneously gives the start-the-clock signal (5). If the previous play was an incomplete forward pass or if the play ended out of bounds, the referee gives the ready-for-play while simultaneously blowing his whistle (6).

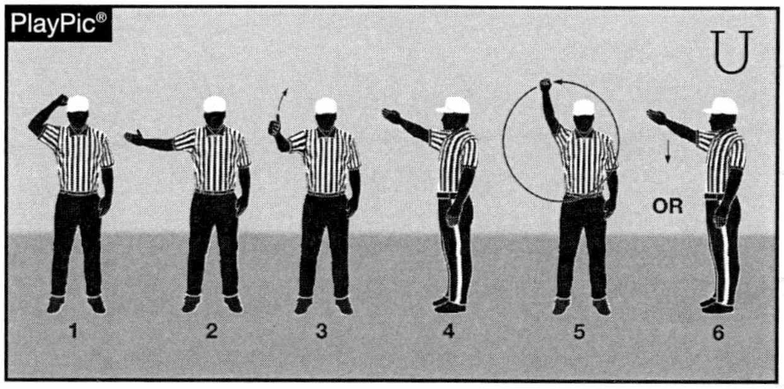

CHAPTER 4

SIGNALING DEAD-BALL FOULS

When a dead-ball foul has been called, the dead-ball signal must precede the signal for the nature of the foul. That means signaling the penalty is a four- or five-step process: the dead-ball signal, followed by the foul signal, followed by a point toward the team that fouled, followed by an indication of the next down, followed by either the ready-for-play or start-the-clock signal.

In PlayPic V, team B has been flagged for a personal foul that occurred during a dead-ball period. The referee begins with the dead-ball signal (1), followed by the signal for personal foul (2). He then indicates the team that fouled (3) and signals the next down. If the penalty results in a first down, the referee signals that team A has been awarded a new series (4); if not, the referee signals the next down. In this example, the penalty has given team A sufficient yardage for a first down. If the previous play ended inbounds, the referee blows his whistle and simultaneously gives the start-the-clock signal (5). If the previous play was an incomplete forward pass or if the play ended out of bounds, the referee gives the ready-for-play while simultaneously blowing his whistle (6).

PENALTY SIGNALING SEQUENCES

Penalties for dead-ball fouls are rarely declined because the yardage is "free." However, on those rare occasions when a dead-ball foul is declined, the referee must indicate the declination after indicating which team fouled.

In PlayPic W on page 34, team K is ready to attempt a try but team R has been called for encroachment. Team K declines the penalty because its kicker is more comfortable kicking from the present distance. The referee gives the signals for dead-ball foul (1) and encroachment (2). He indicates which team has fouled (3), followed by the declination (4). The referee then gives the ready-for-play while simultaneously blowing his whistle (5).

STRAIGHTEN UP!

Posture and body language are important elements in officiating, particularly in signaling. There are a few signals (clipping and blocking below the waist come to mind) that necessitate bending at the waist. But the vast majority of signals should be given standing with a straight back.

PlayPic X illustrates one of the most often "bent over" signals — the one for penalty declined. An official using that posture and moving his arms will look silly. Bending over in that manner should be avoided.

Whether signaling a failed kick attempt, an incomplete pass or declination of a penalty, stand up straight. Do not bend at the waist as shown in the PlayPic.

CHAPTER 5

SPOTS AND THE ALL-BUT-ONE PRINCIPLE

Knowing what acts are fouls, the penalty yardage for those fouls and the proper signal are all important aspects of the penalty procedure. But all of that knowledge is worthless if you don't know the place from where the penalty is to be enforced.

Here is an explanation of terms that will be used throughout this book. They are elementary to penalty enforcement procedures.

STATUS OF THE BALL

In order to properly enforce a penalty, officials must know the status of the ball at the time the foul occurred. There are only two possibilities: It's either a live-ball foul or a dead-ball foul. Dead-ball fouls that prevent the snap (e.g. encroachment, delay of game) are different from dead-ball fouls that occur after the play is over. Unsportsmanlike fouls may occur while the ball is live or while the ball is dead. Whatever the status of the ball, unsportsmanlike fouls are enforced as if they occurred after the play was over.

The ball is dead during the interval between downs. The ball becomes live when the ball has been legally snapped or free kicked and a down is in progress.

When the ball is live, it is either in possession or loose. A loose ball is a pass (forward or backward), a fumble or a kick. Possession is gained when a player takes a snap, catches a pass or kick, recovers a fumble or muff or is handed the ball.

CHAPTER 5

TYPES OF FOULS

A dead-ball foul occurs in the time interval after a down has ended and before the ball again becomes live via a snap or free kick. Conversely, a live-ball foul is one that occurs while a down is in progress. A foul simultaneous with the snap is an act such as illegal motion or illegal formation that becomes a foul when the ball is snapped or free kicked. The ball remains live when a foul simultaneous with the snap occurs.

Most fouls are player fouls, such as holding, encroachment, grasping the facemask, etc. A player is one of the 22 participants on the field. Other individuals, such as coaches, athletic trainers, substitutes, etc., are non-players. Non-player or unsportsmanlike fouls are non-contact fouls.

When the ball is live, one of two types of plays occurs: a loose-ball play or a running play.

A loose-ball play is action during a free kick or scrimmage kick, a legal forward pass, a backward pass (including the snap), an illegal kick or fumble by team A from in or behind the neutral zone prior to a change of team possession. The run or runs that precedes a legal or illegal kick, legal forward pass, backward pass or fumble is considered part of a loose-ball play. For instance, quarterback A1 drops back to pass but has to scramble before throwing a legal forward pass. A2 is flagged for holding during A1's scramble. That is a loose-ball play because the run preceded a legal pass.

A post-scrimmage kick (PSK) foul is a special kind of loose-ball play and has special enforcement. PSK applies to any foul by team R, other than illegal substitution or participation that occurs at the snap that occurs before the kick ends during scrimmage-kick plays other than a try or successful field goal.

The foul must occur beyond the neutral zone during a scrimmage-kick play in which the ball crosses the expanded neutral zone (the neutral zone may be expanded up to two yards behind team R's line of scrimmage). For PSK to apply, team K would not be next to put the ball into play.

Any other play is considered a running play.

SPOTS

The previous spot is just what the name implies — it is the point at which the ball was last put into play, either by a snap or a free kick (see page 21). That is a common enforcement spot, so the crew must know where it is. If there is a foul during a play, the chain crew should not move the down marker so the officials can easily locate the previous spot.

The succeeding spot is the point at which the ball will next be put into play either by a snap or a free kick. It is an important spot for penalty enforcement, because we always step off penalties for dead-ball fouls from that spot. The succeeding spot is most often just the dead-ball spot — the yardline where the ball was declared dead on the play just completed. But the succeeding spot might be somewhere else due to the ball having been relocated by a penalty.

The basic spot is a point of reference for penalty enforcement. For a loose-ball play other than PSK

CHAPTER 5

situations, the basic spot is the previous spot. The basic spot is the end of the run for a running play.

The enforcement spot is the point from which a penalty is enforced.

The dead-ball spot is the spot under the foremost point of the ball when it becomes dead by rule.

The post-scrimmage kick spot is the spot where the kick ends. Team R retains the ball after penalty enforcement from the post-scrimmage kick spot when a post-scrimmage foul occurs. Fouls by team R behind the post-scrimmage kick spot are spot fouls. The spot where the kick ends applies only to PSK. It is the spot during a punt or field-goal attempt at which a player gets possession or the kick is declared dead. If the punt ends in the end zone, the 20 yardline is considered the end of the kick. If team K's punt goes out of bounds or a team R player catches it at team R's 25 yardline, that is the end of the kick. If the ball breaks the plane of team R's goalline, the end of the kick is team R's 20 yardline.

The spot of the foul is the point at which the foul occurred. Because that is such a common enforcement spot, the official calling a foul should drop his flag as close to that point as possible. When a penalty is enforced from that location, it is called a spot foul.

The spot where a run ends could be any of several places. The most obvious is the point at which a runner is tackled or goes out of bounds, or where the ball is otherwise declared dead in his possession. But there are a number of other places where a run ends. For example, a runner might fumble the ball, throw a backward pass or throw an illegal forward pass. The point at which each of those happens is the end of the run. Suppose A1 fumbles the ball at his 20 yardline and the ball is recovered at team A's 30 yardline. The running play includes all of the action while A1 had the ball and during the fumble. The running play ended at team A's 30 yardline, while the run ended at team A's 20 yardline. The same would be true if A1 had thrown a backward pass: The running play would include the action after the ball left his hand until it was caught, recovered or became dead. If the fumble or backward pass were to come into possession of another player, that would be the beginning of another running play. So, there might be several running plays — thus several runs — during any down.

ALL-BUT-ONE PRINCIPLE

For many fouls, the enforcement spot is given as a part of the statement of the penalty. For example, penalties for fouls that occur in conjunction with the snap, such as encroachment, illegal shift and illegal motion are always enforced from the previous spot. But for many fouls, the rulebook refers to the basic spot, not to a specific location on the field. Those penalties are enforced according to the three-and-one principle, also sometimes referred to as the all-but-one principle.

When the statement of the penalty does not specify the enforcement spot, all-but-one determines the spot from which the penalty is stepped off. Key to using that principle is the notion of the basic spot. The basic spot is not a fixed location on the field; rather, it is a benchmark for locating the enforcement spot, and it varies according to the type of play.

The basic spot (except for PSK) can only be either the previous spot or the end of the run; there are no other candidates.

• For running plays in which the run ends beyond the neutral zone, the basic spot is at the end of the run. The same is true for running plays when there is no neutral zone — kick returns, interception returns and other plays involving a change of team possession.

• For running plays on which the run ends behind the neutral zone, the basic spot is the end of the run.

• For legal forward pass plays and for kick plays that do not involve PSK, it is the previous spot.

Depending on which team fouls and where the foul takes place in relation to the basic spot, the penalty is enforced either from or behind the basic spot. There are four scenarios. Either team may commit a foul and that may happen either behind or beyond the basic spot. Two teams plus two locations equal four possibilities. The basic spot is used in three of them and in the other it is enforced from the spot of the foul. Therein lies the all-but-one.

If the team that does not have the ball commits a foul, enforce the penalty from the basic spot regardless of where the foul happens — either behind or beyond the basic spot. If the team in possession commits a foul, the enforcement spot depends on where the foul was committed. If it happens beyond the basic spot, go back to the basic spot for enforcement. But if it occurs behind the basic spot, enforce from the spot of the foul.

Applying the three-and-one principle is easy when you follow the recipe: Where is the basic spot, and where did the foul occur in relation to the basic spot? Answering those questions will allow you to correctly enforce any penalty that is governed by the all-but-one principle.

CHAPTER 6

FOULS ON RUNNING PLAYS

PlayPic®

FOULS ON RUNNING PLAYS

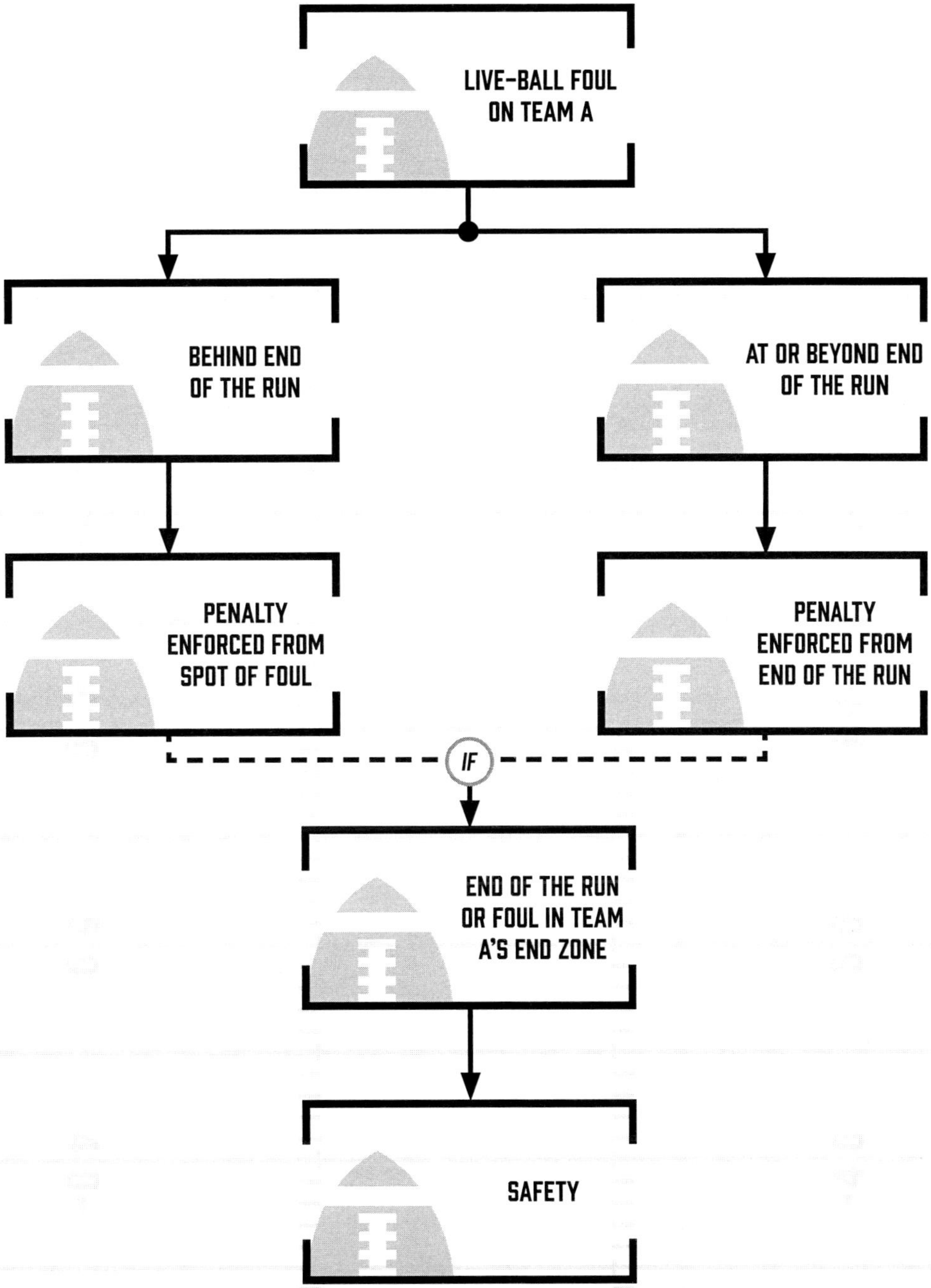

HIGH SCHOOL FOOTBALL PENALTY ENFORCEMENTS · CHAPTER 6

FOULS ON RUNNING PLAYS

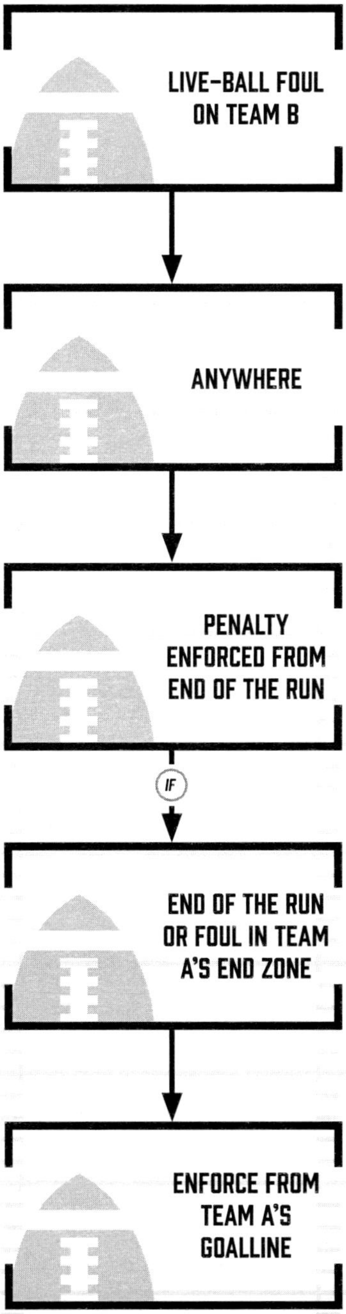

TEAM A FOULS

Any offensive foul on a running play is enforced from the end of the run, unless it is a foul by the offense (team in possession) behind the end of the run. In that case, enforce the penalty from the spot of the foul.

In the plays that follow, it is assumed there are no legal passes or fumbles. Those situations are covered in Chapter 7.

PLAY 1: First and 10 for team A from its own 20 yardline. A1 carries to team A's 35 yardline. A2 is flagged for holding at (a) team A's 25 yardline, or (b) team A's 40 yardline.

RULING 1: All-but-one applies. In (a), enforce the penalty from the spot of the foul. It will be first and 15 from team A's 15 yardline. In (b), the foul occurred beyond the end of the run. Enforce the penalty from the end of the run. It will be first and five from team A's 25 yardline.

If team A's foul occurs in team A's end zone, it is a safety if the penalty is accepted, because the spot of enforcement is behind the goalline.

PLAY 2: First and 10 for team A from its own 15 yardline. A1 drops back to pass. A2 is flagged for holding. The foul occurs (a) at team A's 10 yardline, (b) team A's four yardline, or (c) in team A's end zone. A1 is downed at his own six yardline.

RULING 2: In (a), if team B accepts the penalty, it is enforced half the distance from the end of the run. It will be first and 22 from team A's three yardline. In (b), if team B accepts the penalty, it is enforced half the distance from the spot of the foul. That yields first and 23 from team A's two yardline. In (c), if team B accepts the penalty, it scores a safety. In (a), (b) and (c), if team B declines, it will be second and 19 for team A from its own six yardline.

ILLEGAL FORWARD PASSES

Under NFHS enforcement, illegal forward passes thrown from behind the line are fouls during running plays and fall under the all-but-one principle. Those penalties are enforced from the spot of the foul. The penalty includes a loss of down. If the spot of the foul is in team A's end zone, it is a safety whether or not team B accepts the penalty.

If an ineligible team A player muffs, bats or catches a pass behind the line, it is illegal touching, not an illegal pass. That is a five-yard penalty enforced from the spot of the foul and includes loss of down. If the spot of the foul is in team A's end zone, it is a safety if team B accepts the penalty.

Illegal forward passes thrown beyond the line are also considered running plays. The five-yard penalty is enforced from the spot of the foul and includes a loss of down. The best way to remember that is to give the runner the yardage gained legally before the pass.

Note that pass interference and roughing the passer are not possible when a pass is illegal, but the contact can be ruled a personal foul.

If team B fouls during a down that includes an illegal forward pass, the penalties cancel.

PLAY 3: First and 10 for team A from its own 10 yardline. A1 throws an illegal forward pass that falls incomplete. The pass is thrown (a) from team A's end zone, (b) at team A's six yardline, or (c) at team A's 22 yardline.

RULING 3: In (a), team B will score a safety whether or not it accepts the penalty. In (b) and (c), the penalty is enforced from the spot of the illegal pass and includes a loss of down. That yields second and 17 from team A's three yardline in (b) and second and three from team A's 17 yardline in (c).

PLAY 4: Third and 10 on team A's 10 yardline. A1 is sacked in his end zone, but A2 holds on his own six yardline.

RULING 4: Declining the penalty and accepting the result of the play gives team B a safety. Because the end of the run is behind the spot of the foul, enforcement would be from within team A's end zone. Thus accepting the penalty would give team B a safety as well.

Fouls by team A in team B's end zone prior to a touchdown by team A are enforced from the goalline, because the goalline is the end of the run.

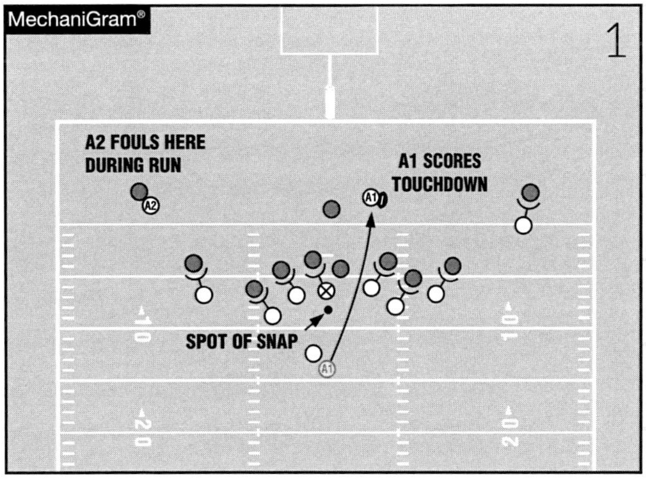

PLAY 5: As seen in MechaniGram 1, it is

first and goal for team A from team B's eight yardline. A1 runs for a touchdown. During the run, A2 is flagged for holding in team B's end zone.

RULING 5: The penalty is enforced from team B's goalline. It will be first and goal from team B's 10 yardline.

TEAM B FOULS

The basic rule is to enforce any defensive foul on a running play from the end of the run, producing what is often referred to as a "tack-on."

PLAY 6: First and 10 for team A from its own 20 yardline. A1 carries to team A's 35 yardline. B2 is flagged for grabbing but not twisting A3's facemask. The foul occurs at (a) team A's 25 yardline, or (b) team A's 40 yardline.

RULING 6: In (a) and (b), the penalty is enforced from the end of the run. It will be first and 10 from team A's 40 yardline.

FOULS AT THE SNAP

Fouls at the snap include illegal motion, illegal formation and illegal shift. Those fouls are enforced from the previous spot and the down is repeated.

PLAY 7: First and 10 for team A from its own 20 yardline. A1 carries to team A's 35 yardline. At the snap, team A is flagged for failing to have at least seven players on the line of scrimmage.

RULING 7: Team B will undoubtedly accept the penalty. The penalty is enforced from the previous spot. It will be first and 15 from team A's 15 yardline.

LIVE-BALL FOULS ENFORCED AS DEAD-BALL FOULS

All live-ball fouls enforced as dead-ball fouls are enforced in the same fashion as dead-ball fouls.

PLAY 8: As seen in MechaniGram 2, it is first and 10 for team A from its own 20 yardline. A1 carries to team A's 30 yardline. During the play, team B's coach is flagged for being outside the restricted area.

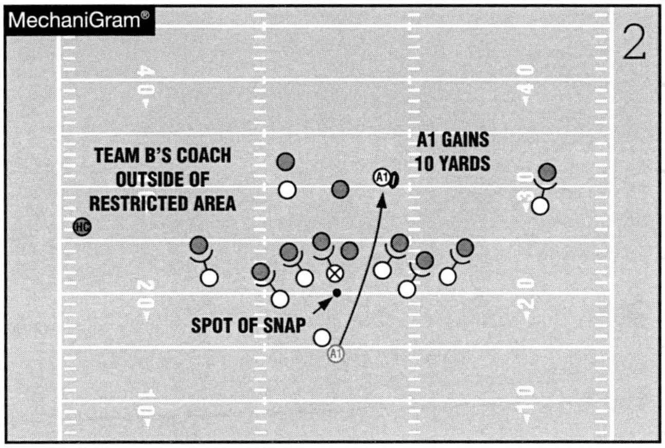

RULING 8: Although the foul occurred while the ball was live, unsportsmanlike conduct is a live-ball foul treated as a dead-ball foul. Team A will undoubtedly accept the penalty, which is enforced from the end of A1's run. The result is first and 10 from team A's 45 yardline.

CHAPTER 7

FOULS DURING A BACKWARD PASS, FUMBLE OR LEGAL FORWARD PASS

PlayPic®

FOULS DURING A BACKWARD PASS, FUMBLE OR LEGAL FORWARD PASS

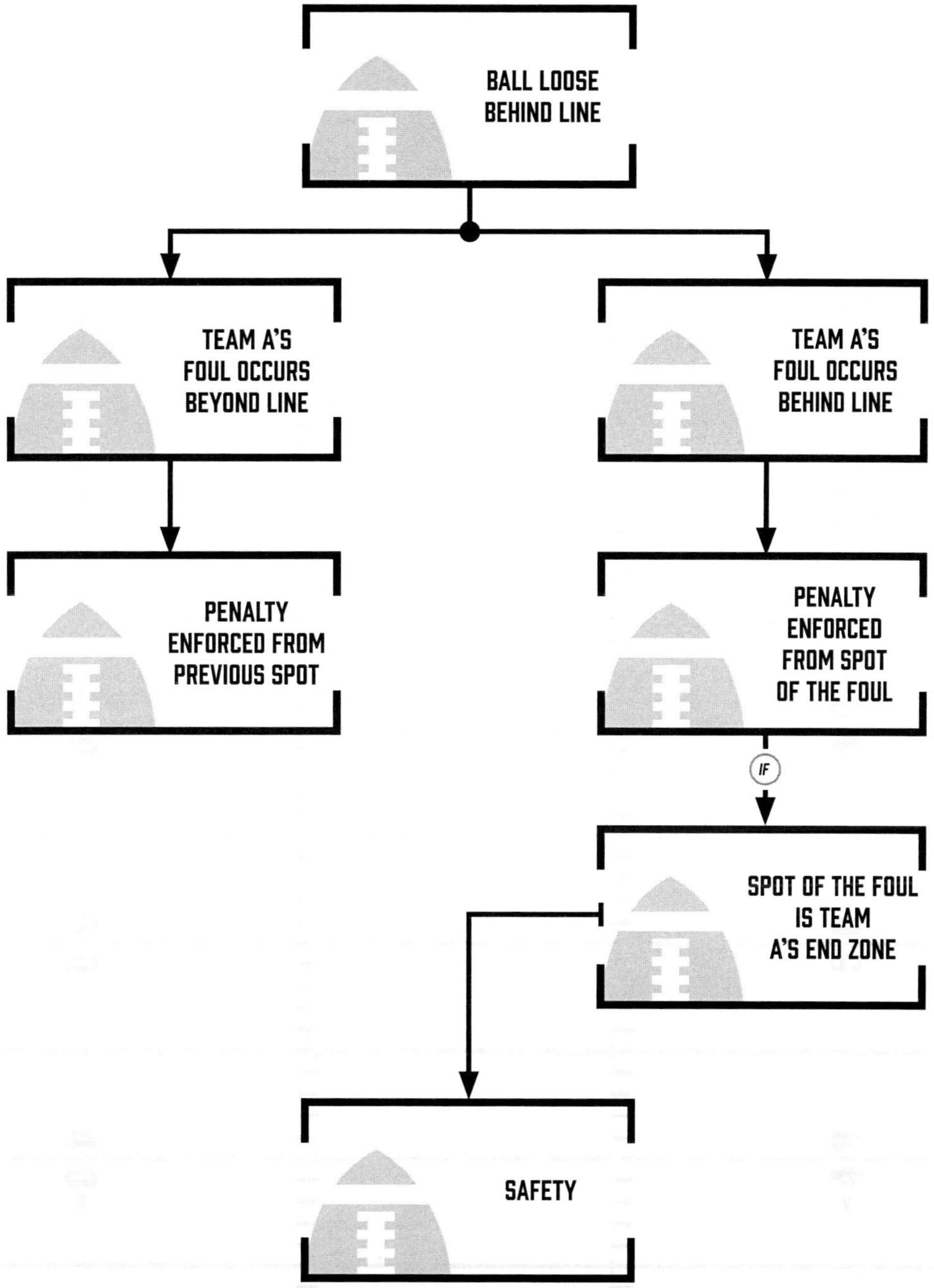

FOULS DURING A BACKWARD PASS, FUMBLE OR LEGAL FORWARD PASS

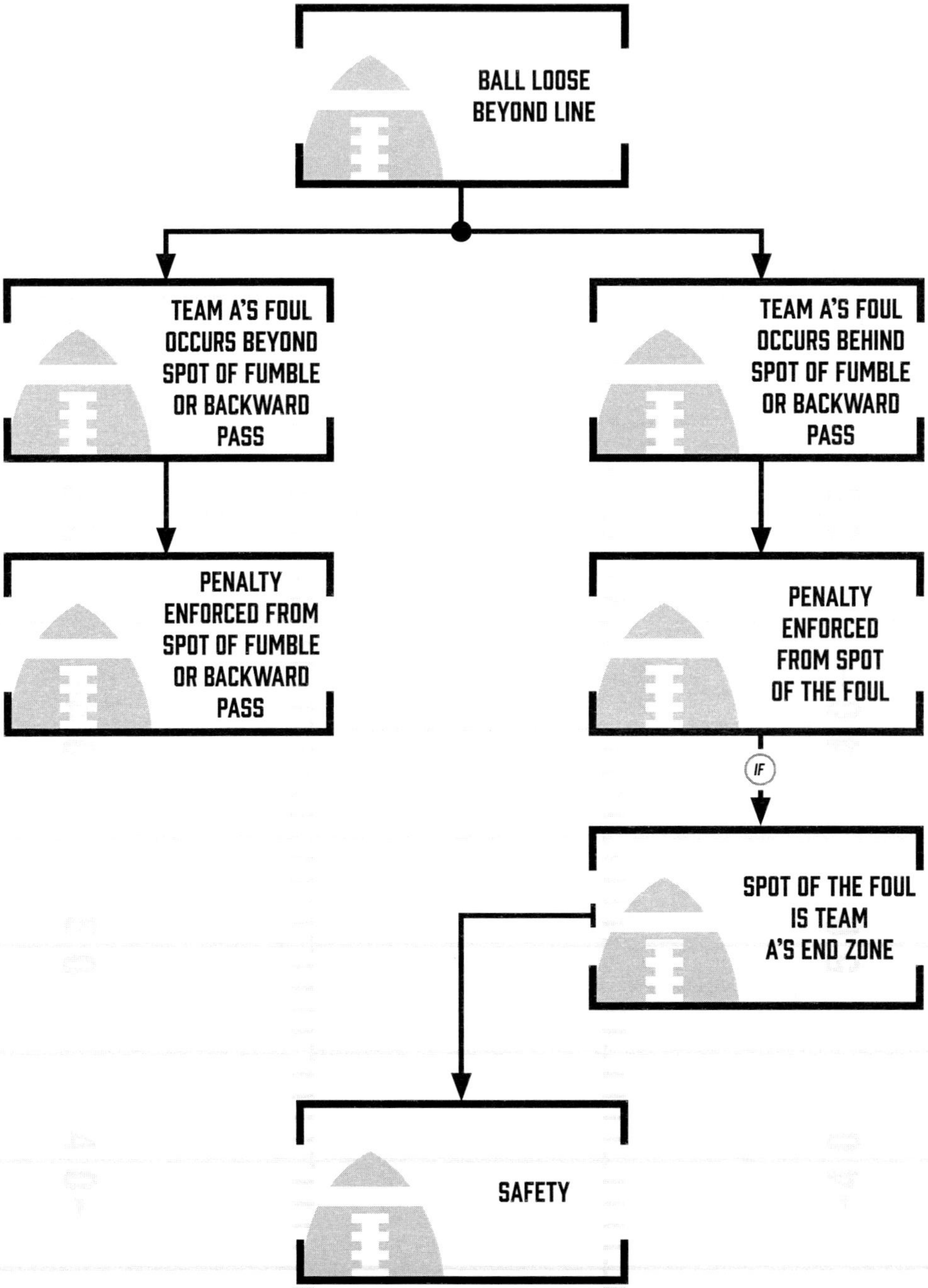

ROUGHING THE PASSER ON LEGAL FORWARD PASS

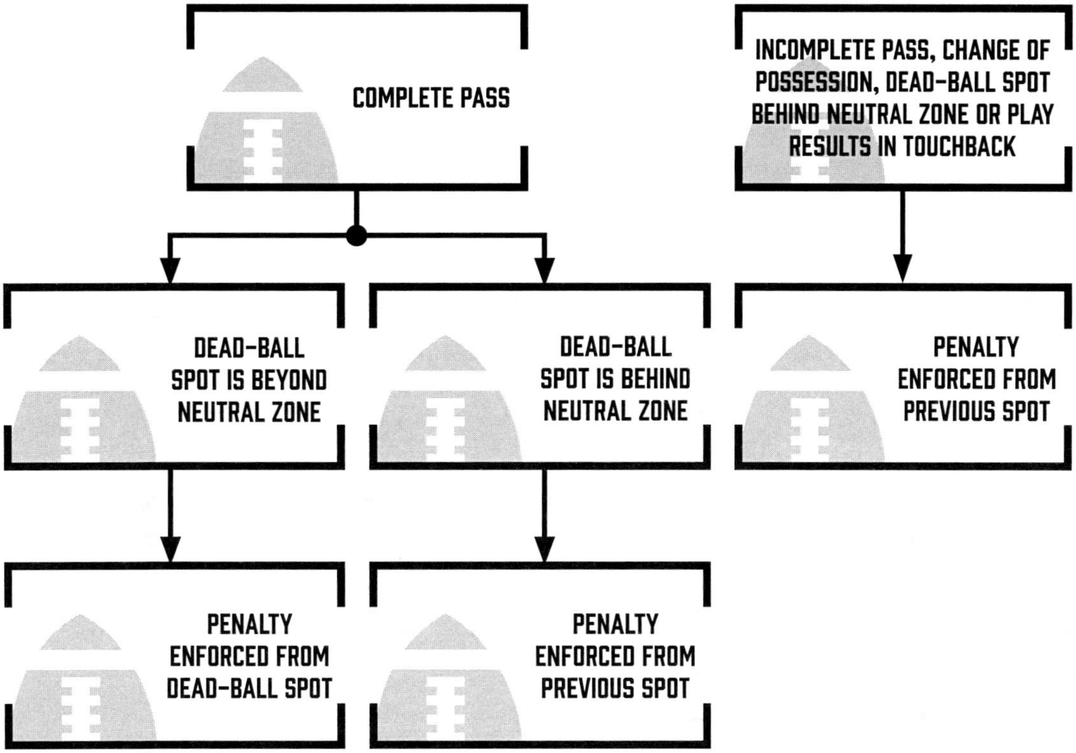

OTHER TEAM B FOULS DURING A BACKWARD PASS, FUMBLE OR LEGAL FORWARD PASS

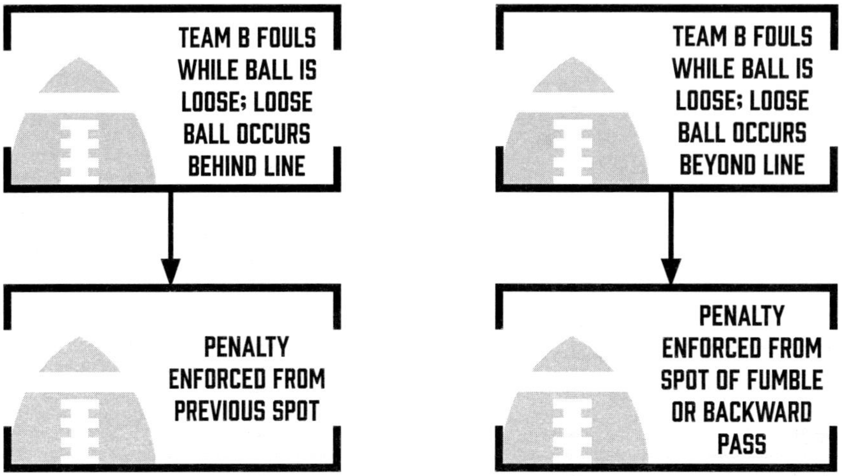

FOULS DURING A BACKWARD PASS, FUMBLE OR FORWARD PASS

Fouls during plays that involve passes are generally enforced from the previous spot. Remember, the "pass play" begins with the snap and is over when the pass is caught or incomplete.

In the plays that follow, it is assumed there are no illegal passes. Those situations are covered in Chapter 6.

PLAY 1: First and 10 for team A from its own 30 yardline. A1's legal forward pass is incomplete beyond the line. Holding is called at team A's 45 yardline on (a) A2, or (b) B3.

RULING 1: In either case, the penalty is enforced from the previous spot. In (a), it will be first and 20 for team A from its own 20 yardline. In (b), it will be first and 10 for team A from its own 40 yardline.

PLAY 2: First and 10 for team A from its own 30 yardline. A1's legal forward pass is incomplete. Holding is called on (a) A1, or (b) B2. The foul occurs at team A's 25 yardline.

RULING 2: The previous spot is the basic spot. In (a), since the team A foul occurred behind the basic spot, the all-but-one principle applies and the penalty is enforced from the spot of the foul. It will be first and 25 for team A from its own 15 yardline. In (b), the penalty for team B's foul is enforced from the previous spot. It will be first and 10 for team A from its own 40 yardline.

CHAPTER 7

Penalties for roughing the passer on a completed forward pass are enforced from the dead-ball spot when the dead-ball spot is beyond neutral zone and there is no change of team possession during the down. If there is a change of possession during the down, if the dead-ball spot is behind the neutral zone or if the result of the play is a touchback, enforce from the previous spot.

PLAY 3: First and 10 for team A from its own 20 yardline. A1's screen pass is caught by A2 at team A's 18 yardline, where he is immediately tackled. B3 is flagged for roughing the passer.

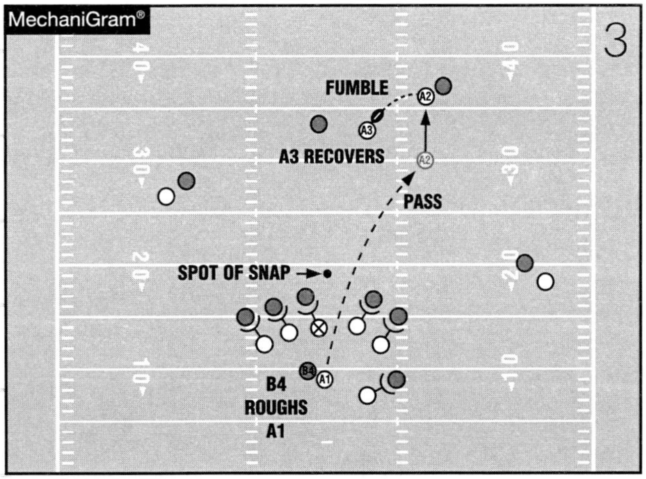

RULING 3: Because the dead-ball spot is behind the neutral zone, the penalty is enforced from the previous spot. It will be team A's ball, first and 10 at its own 35 yardline.

PLAY 4: As seen in MechaniGram 3, it's first and 10 for team A from its own 20 yardline. A1's pass is caught by A2 at team A's 30 yardline. A2 fumbles at team A's 35 yardline. Prone A3 recovers at team A's 33 yardline. B4 is flagged for roughing the passer.

RULING 4: In that case, the penalty is enforced from the dead-ball spot — the spot where A3 recovers. It will be team A's ball, first and 10 at its 48 yardline.

FOULS DURING A BACKWARD PASS, FUMBLE OR FORWARD PASS

PLAY 5: First and 10 for team A from team B's 20 yardline. A1's pass is caught by A2 at team B's 10 yardline. A2 fumbles and prone B3 recovers at (a) team B's eight yardline, or (b) in team B's end zone. B4 is flagged for roughing the passer.

RULING 5: In both (a) and (b), a change of possession has occurred. As a result, the penalty is enforced from the previous spot. It will be team A's ball, first and goal at team B's 10 yardline.

The basic spot for penalties on loose-ball plays is the previous spot. A loose-ball play includes action during:

- A legal forward pass.
- A backward pass (including the snap), illegal kick or fumble made by team A from in or behind the neutral zone prior to a change of team possession.
- Any run that precedes such legal or illegal kick, legal forward pass, backward pass or fumble.

TEAM A FOULS

If a fumble, backward pass or legal forward pass occurs behind the neutral zone, the basic spot is the previous spot. Fouls by team A behind the basic spot are enforced from the spot of the foul. If the foul occurs in team A's end zone, it is a safety if team B accepts the penalty.

If a fumble, backward pass or legal forward pass occurs behind the neutral zone and team A fouls beyond the neutral zone, enforce team A's foul from the previous spot.

CHAPTER 7

If a fumble or backward pass occurs beyond the neutral zone and team A fouls behind the spot of the backward pass or fumble, enforce team A's foul from the spot of the foul. If the foul occurs in team A's end zone, it is a safety if team B accepts the penalty.

If a fumble or backward pass occurs beyond the neutral zone and team A fouls beyond the spot of the backward pass or fumble, it is a running play. Enforce the penalty for team A's foul from the spot of the fumble or backward pass.

If a fumble, backward pass or legal forward pass occurs behind the neutral zone, enforce all team B fouls occurring before or while the ball is loose from the previous spot.

If a fumble or backward pass occurs beyond the neutral zone, enforce all team B fouls occurring before or while the ball is loose from the spot of the fumble or backward pass.

PLAY 6: First and 10 for team A from its own 20 yardline. A1's run results in a five-yard gain, but he fumbles. While the ball is loose, B2 holds A3 at team A's (a) 30 yardline, or (b) 10 yardline. A4 recovers the loose ball and advances to the 50 yardline.

RULING 6: In (a) and (b), B2's foul cannot be tacked on at the end of the run, even though team A recovered its own fumble, because the spot of enforcement would be the spot of A1's fumble. Team A will likely decline the penalty in (a) and (b) and begin a new series at the 50 yardline. If team A accepted the penalty in (a) or (b), it would be enforced from the end of A1's run (team A's 25 yardline).

FOULS DURING A BACKWARD PASS, FUMBLE OR FORWARD PASS

The basic spot for fouls by team A during a loose-ball play is the previous spot.

PLAY 7: First and 10 for team A from team A's 10 yardline. A1 drops back into his own end zone to pass, but he is hit and fumbles. While the ball is loose, A2 holds B3 (a) at team A's four yardline, (b) at team A's 18 yardline, or (c) in team A's end zone. A1 recovers the loose ball and advances to team A's 15 yardline.

RULING 7: In all three cases, the basic spot is the previous spot because the fumble occurred behind the line. In (a), because the spot of the foul is behind the basic spot, if the penalty is accepted, it is enforced from the spot of the foul. The result is first and 18 for team A from its two yardline. In (b), because the foul occurred beyond the basic spot, the penalty is enforced from the basic spot. If the penalty is accepted, it will be first and 15 for team A from its five yardline. In (c), the foul occurred in team A's end zone. If the penalty is accepted, the result is a safety.

CHANGE OF POSSESSION, RUN ENDS IN END ZONE

The basic spot is the 20 yardline for fouls by the opponent of the team in possession at the time of the foul when the opponent is responsible for forcing the ball across the goalline of the team in possession and the result of the play is a touchback, or the run ends in the end zone and is followed by a loose ball.

CHAPTER 7

The basic spot is the goalline for fouls by the opponent of the team in possession at the time of the foul when the team in possession is responsible for forcing the ball across the goalline of the team in possession and the result of the play is a safety, or the run ends in the end zone and is followed by a loose ball.

PLAY 8: As seen in MechaniGram 4, A1's legal forward pass is intercepted by B2, who is in his own end zone and attempts to advance. A4 grabs but does not twist B2's facemask.

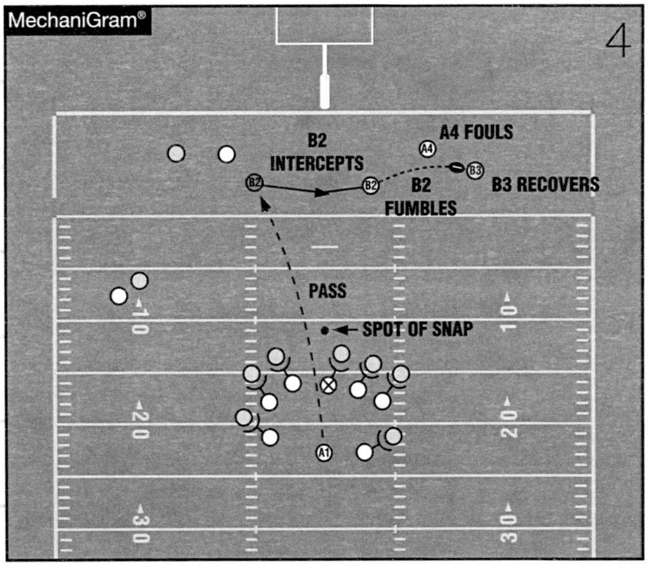

B2 fumbles while still in his own end zone. Prone B3 recovers the ball in the end zone.

RULING 8: The related run ended in team B's end zone. If accepted, the penalty is enforced from the basic spot (team B's 20 yardline). The result is first and 10 for team B from its 25 yardline.

PLAY 9: As seen in MechaniGram 5 on page 63, B1 intercepts A1's pass at his own six yardline. B1 retreats into his own end zone, but before he can bring the ball across the goalline, his facemask is grabbed but not twisted by A2. B1 fumbles and the ball rolls out of bounds at team B's three yardline.

RULING 9: Because the related run ended in team B's end zone and the team in possession was responsible for the force, the basic spot is team B's goalline. Team B will likely accept the penalty, which results in first and 10 for team B from its five yardline.

PLAY 10: B1 intercepts a pass in his own end zone and advances to team B's six yardline, where he is hit and fumbles. Prone B2 recovers (a) at team B's four yardline, or (b) in team B's end zone. While the ball is loose, B3 holds at team B's four yardline.

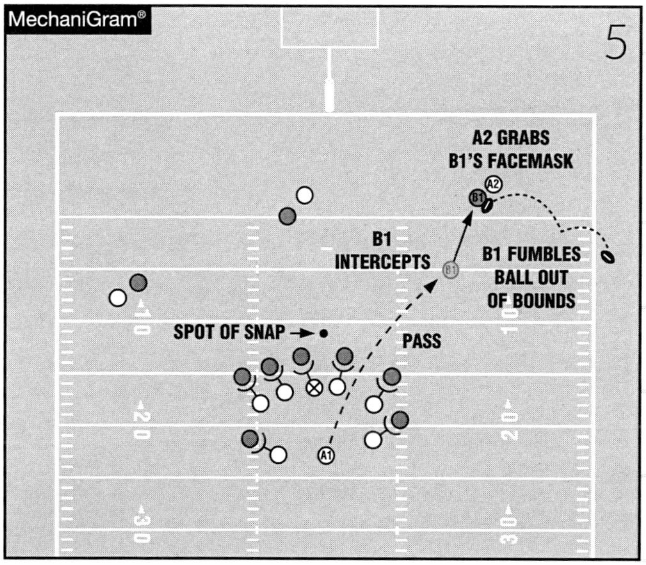

RULING 10: In both cases, the basic spot is the end of the run (the spot of B1's fumble). If team A accepts the penalty, it is enforced from the basic spot. In (a), that yields first and 10 for team B from its own two yardline. However, in (b), if team A declines the penalty, it scores a safety. B1's fumble was the force that put the ball in team B's end zone.

CHAPTER 8

FOULS ON FREE-KICK PLAYS

PlayPic®

FOULS ON FREE-KICK PLAYS

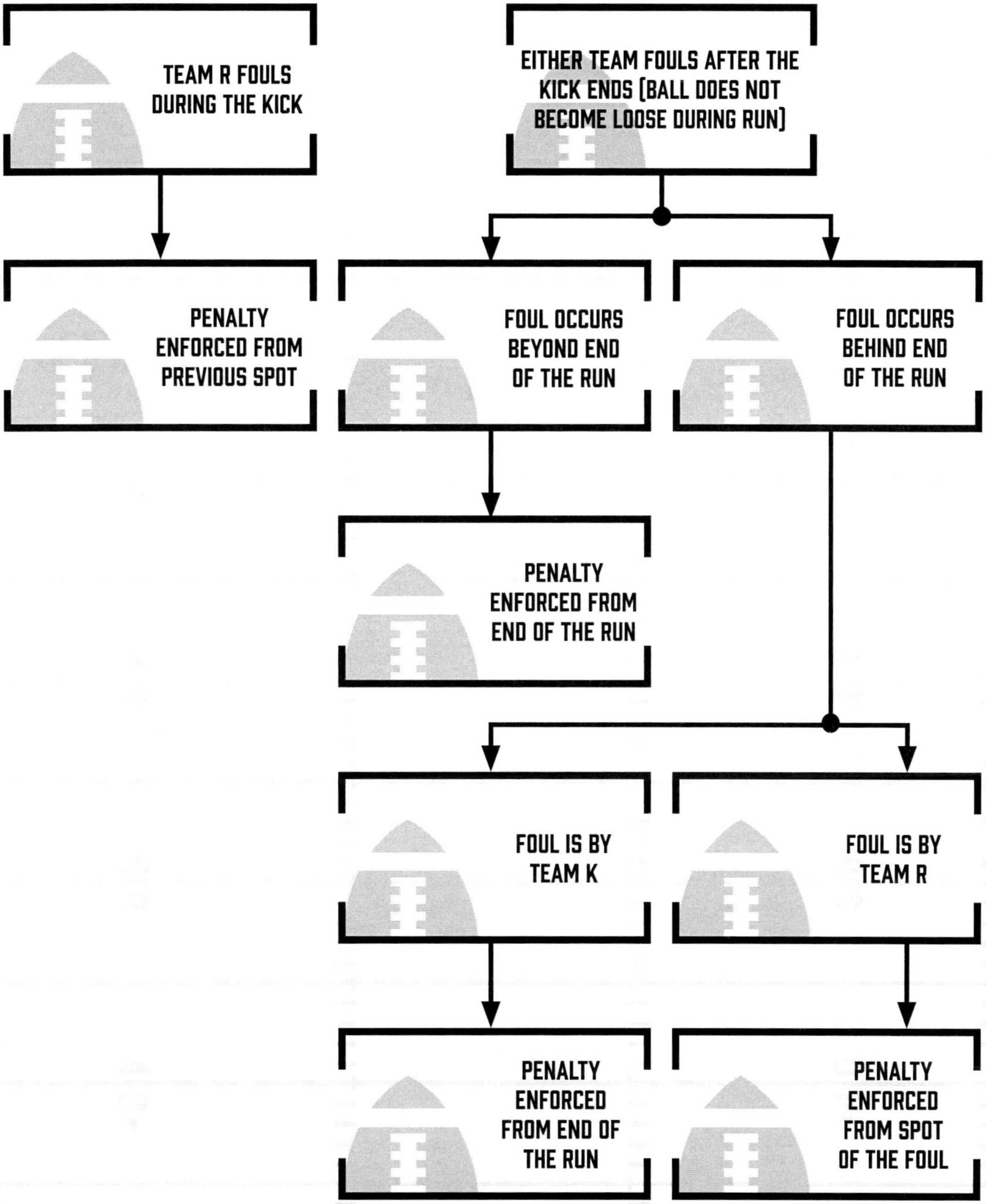

FOULS ON FREE-KICK PLAYS

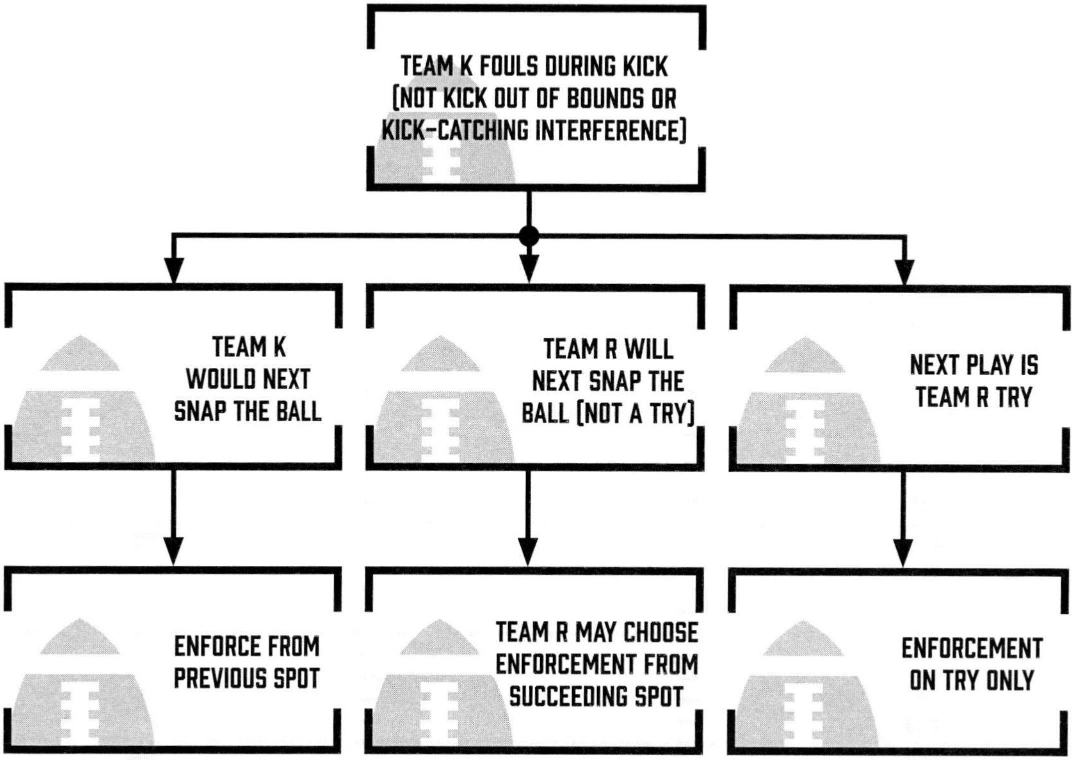

NOTE 1: Team R options on kick-catching interference:

- *Accept the results of the play*
- *Accept an awarded fair catch after enforcement of a 15-yard penalty from the spot of the foul*
- *Accept a 15-yard penalty from the previous spot and a replay of the down*

NOTE 2: Team R options on free kick out of bounds:

- *Accept 5-yard penalty from the succeeding spot*
- *Put the ball in play at the inbounds spot 25 yards beyond the previous spot if the previous spot is on the midfield side of team R's 25 yardline from the spot of the foul*
- *Accept a 5-yard penalty from the previous spot and a replay of the down*

If team K commits a foul other than kick-catching interference during a free kick down and will not be next to put the ball in play, team R may choose to have the penalty enforced from the succeeding spot or at the previous spot. If team K would next put the ball in the play, the penalty is enforced at the previous spot.

PLAY 1: While K1's free kick is in flight, K2 grasps and twists R3's facemask. The ball is caught by R4, who returns it to team R's 25 yardline.

RULING 1: Team R may accept a 15-yard penalty from the previous spot and have team K rekick, or accept enforcement of a 15-yard penalty from the end of the play. That would give team R first and 10 at its own 40 yardline.

PLAY 2: While K1's free kick is in flight, K2 grasps and twists R3's facemask. The kick is caught by R4 at his 10 yardline and returned to team R's 20 yardline, where R4 is hit and fumbles. The ball is recovered at team R's 25 yardline by (a) R3, or (b) K4.

RULING 2: In (a), the penalty is enforced from the end of the play. That gives team R a first down at team K's 40 yardline. In (b), in order to negate the loss of possession, team R must accept enforcement from the previous spot.

If team K scores on the kick down, the penalty may only be enforced on the try. There is no enforcement provision for giving the scoring team an option to enforce a penalty on the succeeding kickoff on a change-of-possession play when the foul occurs before the change of possession.

CHAPTER 8

PLAY 3: While K1's free kick is in flight, K2 grasps and twists R3's facemask. The kick is caught by R4 at his 10 yardline and advanced across team K's goalline.

RULING 3: The half-the-distance penalty will be enforced on the try.

The enforcement spot for loose-ball fouls by team R during a free kick is the previous spot.

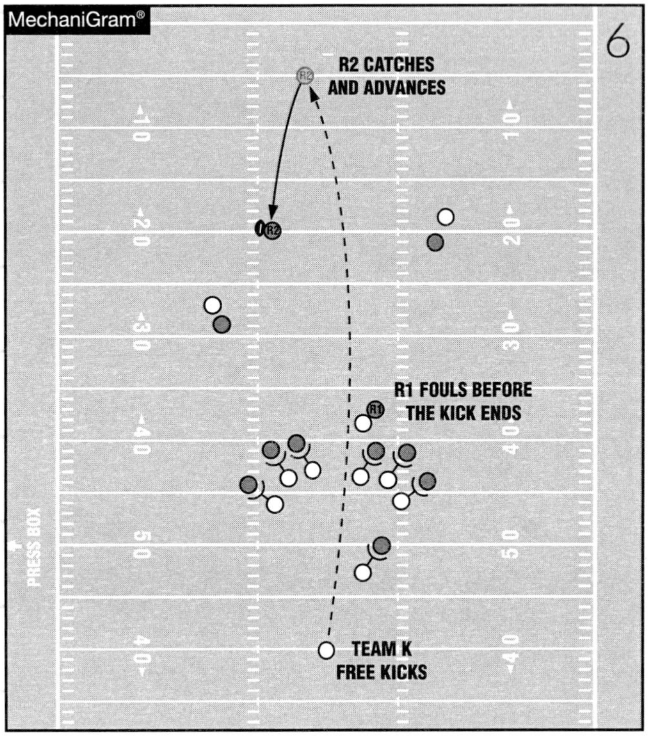

PLAY 4: As seen in MechaniGram 6, team K free kicks from its own 40 yardline. R1 holds while the ball is in flight. R2 catches the ball on team R's five yardline and returns it to team R's 20 yardline.

RULING 4: If the penalty is accepted, team K will rekick after the 10-yard penalty is enforced from the previous spot. If team K declines, it's team R's ball, first and 10 at team R's 20 yardline.

The enforcement spot for fouls that occur after the kick ends when there is no subsequent loose ball (possession has been gained by team R) is the spot of the foul or the end of the run (all-but-one), because those are fouls on running plays.

PLAY 5: Team K free kicks from its own 40 yardline. R5 catches the kick on his own five yardline and returns it to team R's 40 yardline. During the run, R6 clips at team R's 20 yardline.

RULING 5: Fouls that occur after team R recovers or catches the free kick are fouls during a running play. Enforce team R's foul from the spot of the foul because it's behind the end of the run. The half-the-distance penalty yields first and 10 at team R's 10 yardline.

If team K is guilty of kick-catching interference, team R may take an awarded fair catch at the spot of the foul, have team K rekick after enforcement of a 15-yard penalty from the previous spot, or take an awarded fair catch with an additional 15-yard penalty.

FREE KICK OUT OF BOUNDS

When a free kick goes out of bounds untouched inbounds by team R, it is a foul by team K. Team R has four choices: accept a five-yard penalty from the previous spot and have team K rekick; put the ball in play at the inbounds spot 25 yards beyond the previous spot; decline the penalty and put the ball in play at the inbounds spot; or accept a five-yard penalty enforced from the dead-ball spot.

PLAY 6: Team K's free kick from its 40 yardline goes out of bounds untouched at team R's 20 yardline.

RULING 6: If team R chooses previous-spot enforcement, team K will rekick from its own 35 yardline. Choosing to put the ball in play 25 yards beyond the previous spot would yield a new series for team R at its own 35 yardline. Accepting a five-yard penalty enforced from the dead-ball spot would result in a snap from team R's 25 yardline.

BOTH TEAMS FOUL

When both teams commit a live-ball foul (other than non-player or unsportsmanlike) during a down, it is called a double foul. If a double foul occurs during a change-of-possession down and the team in final possession gets the ball free of a foul, it has the opportunity to retain possession. That is known as the "clean hands rule."

PLAY 7: While a free kick is in flight, K1 grabs R2's facemask and R3 clips K4. R5 catches the kick on his own five yardline and returns it to team R's 40 yardline.

RULING 7: Both fouls occurred before the change of possession, so there is no option: The penalties cancel. Team K will rekick from its own 40 yardline.

However, when the "clean hands" team retains possession by declining the opponent's foul, the penalty for the opponent's foul may be enforced.

PLAY 8: As seen in MechaniGram 7, team K free kicks. While the ball is in flight, K1 grabs R1's facemask. R5 catches the kick on his own five yardline and returns it to team R's 20 yardline. During the run, R2 clips at team R's 14 yardline.

RULING 8: Team R gained possession with "clean hands," so it can decline team K's foul. Team K would accept the penalty for team R's foul, which is enforced from the spot of the foul. Due to half-the-distance enforcement, that would result in first and 10 for team A from its own seven yardline. If team R accepts the penalty for team K's foul, the down is replayed.

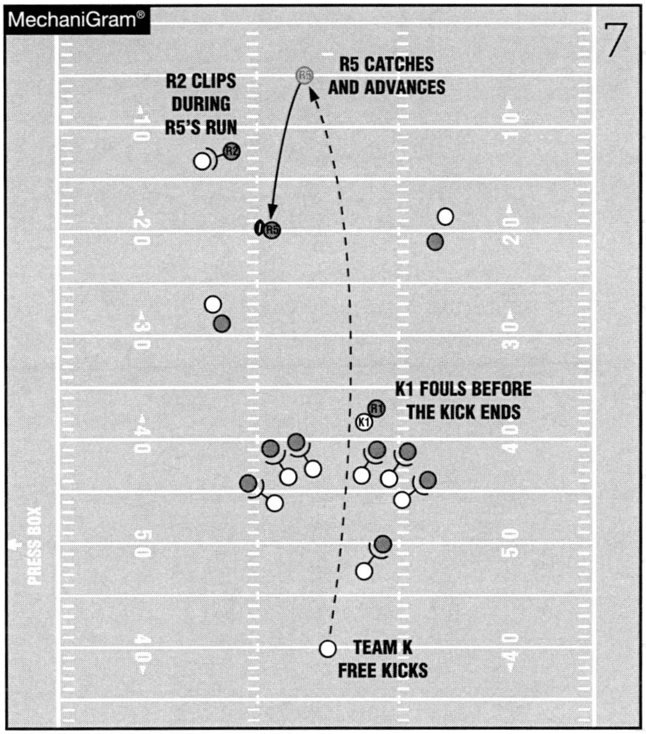

CHAPTER 9

FOULS ON CHANGE OF POSSESSION PLAYS

FOULS ON CHANGE OF POSSESSION PLAYS

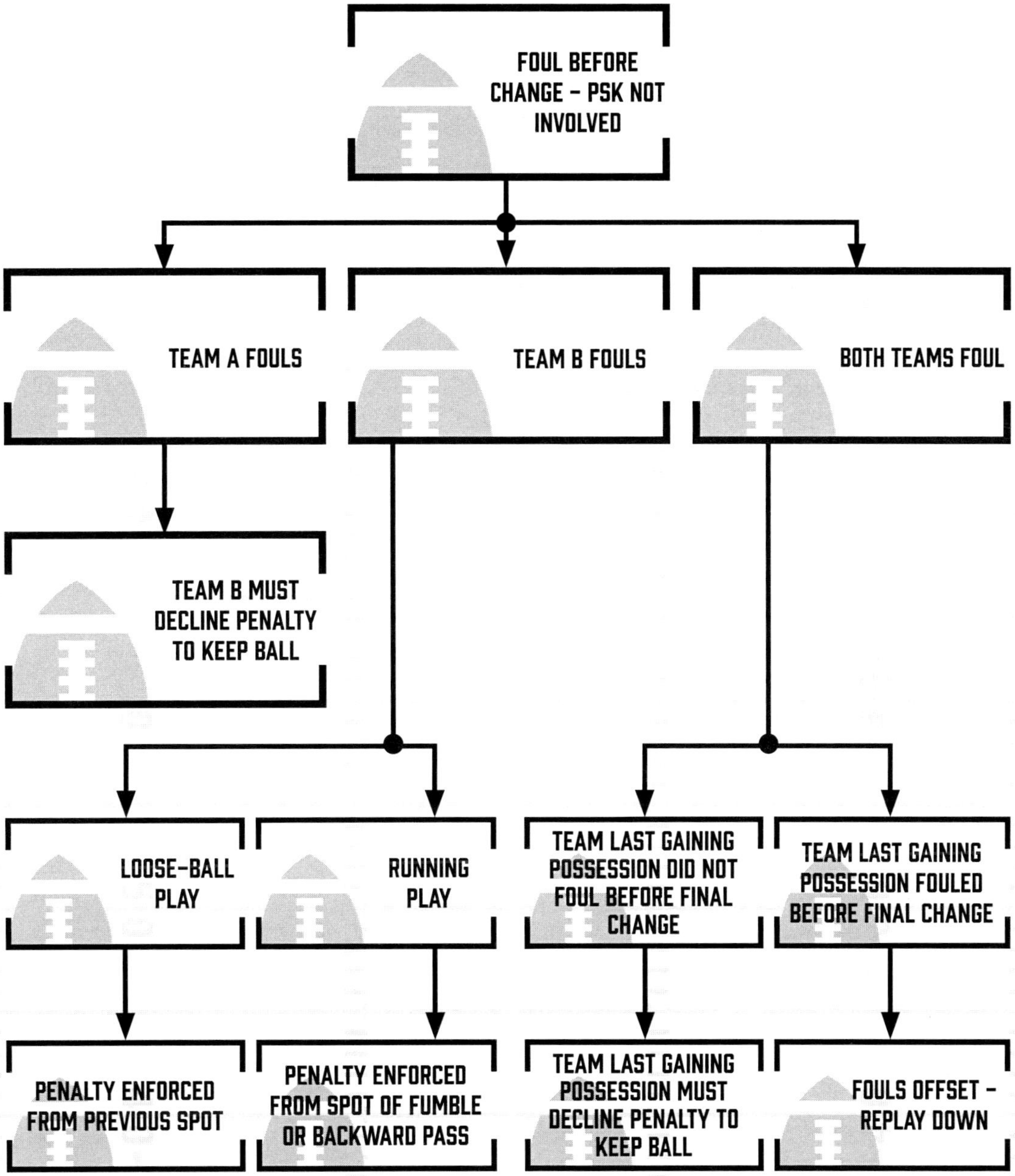

FOULS ON CHANGE OF POSSESSION PLAYS

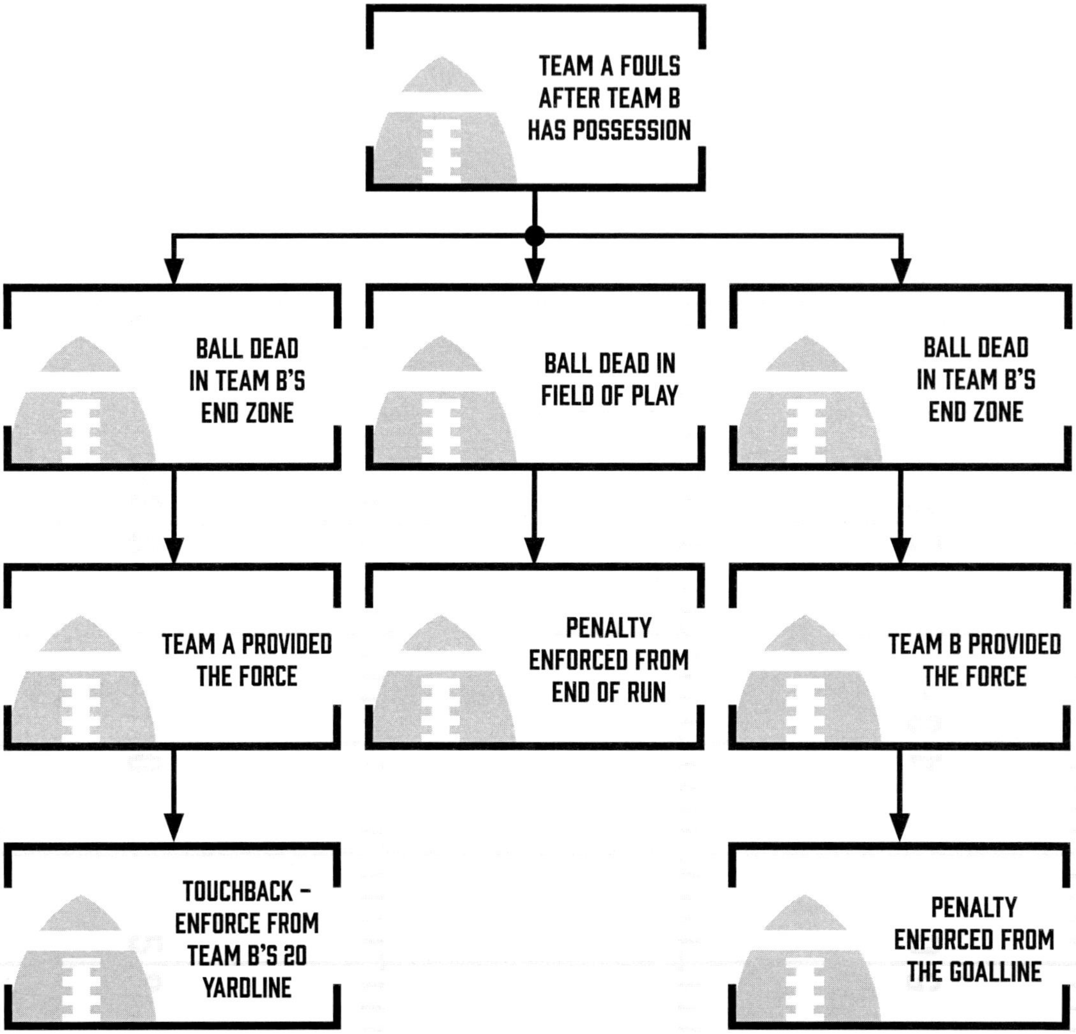

FOULS ON CHANGE OF POSSESSION PLAYS

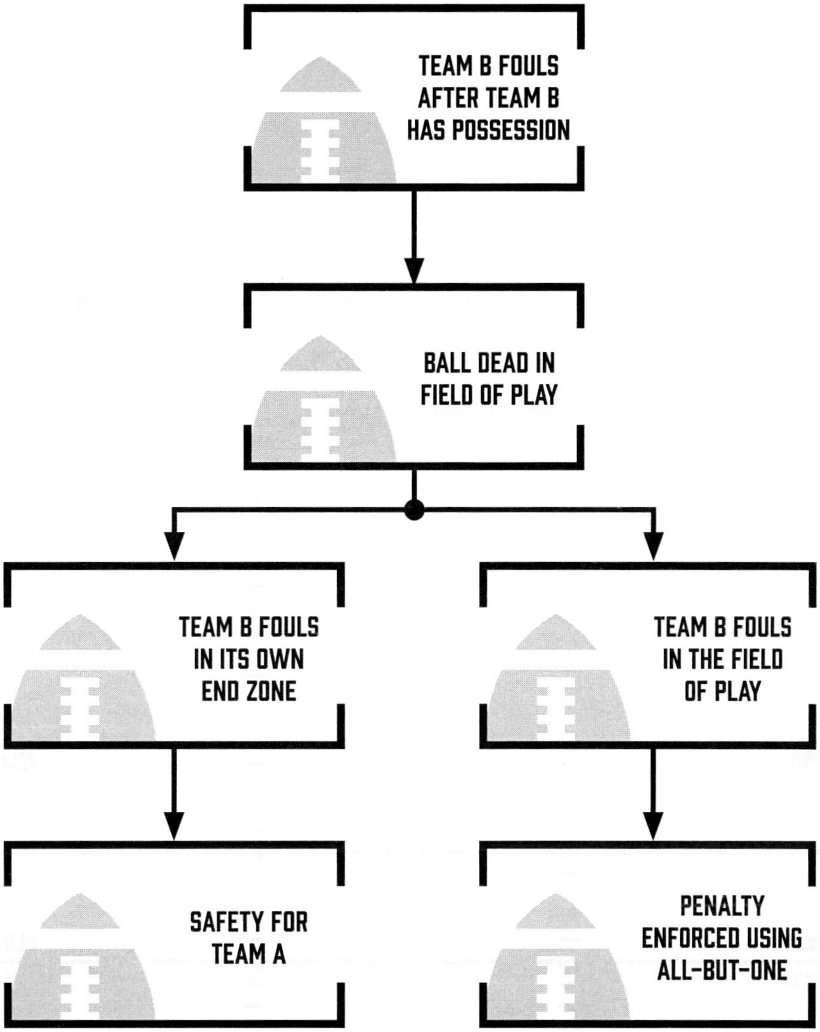

FOULS ON CHANGE OF POSSESSION PLAYS

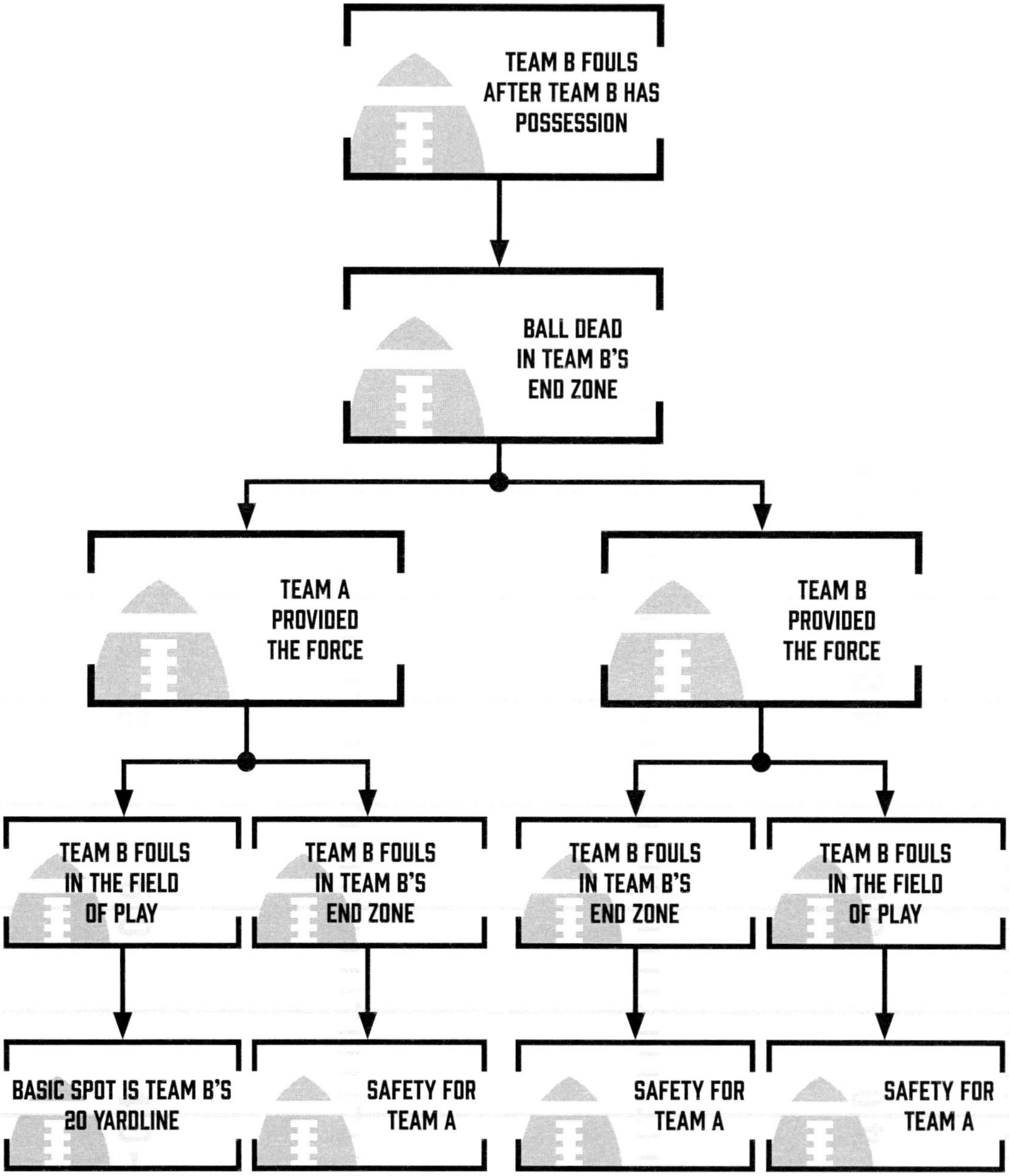

FOULS ON CHANGE OF POSSESSION PLAYS

FOULS DURING A RUN FOLLOWED BY A CHANGE OF TEAM POSSESSION

If team A commits a foul during a running play prior to a change of possession (e.g. fumble or backward pass), team B must decline team A's foul in order to keep the ball.

PLAY 1: First and 10 for team A from its own 20 yardline. A1 has the ball at team A's 25 yardline when A2 holds at team A's 22 yardline. A1 fumbles and B3 recovers at team A's 30 yardline.

RULING 1: Team B must decline the penalty to keep the ball. It will be team B's ball, first and 10 from team A's 30 yardline.

If team B fouls prior to the change of possession, the ball is returned to team A and the penalty for team B's foul is enforced from the spot of the fumble or backward pass.

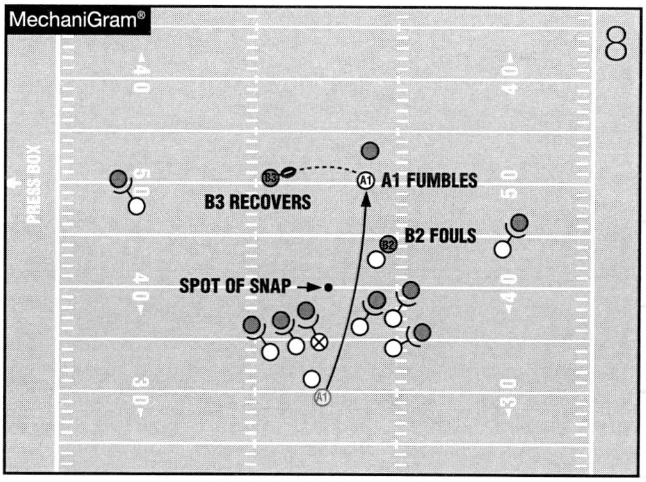

PLAY 2: As seen in MechaniGram 8, it is first and 10 for team A from its own 40 yardline. A1 advances the ball to team A's 45 yardline when B2 grabs and twists A1's facemask. A1 reaches the 50 yardline and fumbles, where prone B3 recovers the loose ball.

RULING 2: Because team B fouled prior to gaining possession, it cannot keep the ball. The ball is returned to team A and the penalty is enforced from the spot of the fumble. It will be team A's ball, first and 10 from team B's 35 yardline.

If team B's foul occurs while team A's fumble or backward pass is behind the line of scrimmage, the enforcement spot is the previous spot.

PLAY 3: First and 10 for team A from its own 20 yardline. Quarterback A1 drops back to pass and is at his own 14 yardline when he fumbles. While the ball is loose, B2 grabs and twists A1's facemask. B3 recovers at team A's 15 yardline.

RULING 3: Because team B fouled prior to gaining possession, it cannot keep the ball. The ball is returned to team A, and the penalty is enforced from the previous spot. It will be team A's ball, first 10 from its own 35 yardline.

EACH TEAM FOULS

If each team fouls during a down in which there is a change of team possession and the play does not involve PSK, the team last gaining possession may retain the ball. In order for that to happen, the team last in possession may not have fouled before the final change of possession (clean hands) and it must decline the penalty for its opponent's foul (other than a nonplayer or unsportsmanlike). For plays that involve PSK, see Chapter 10.

FOULS ON CHANGE OF POSSESSION PLAYS

PLAY 4: First and 10 for team A from its own 20 yardline. Team A is illegally in motion at the snap. A1's legal forward pass is intercepted by B2 at team A's 40 yardline. B2 advances to team A's 20 yardline. During B2's run, B3 is flagged for clipping at team A's 30 yardline.

RULING 4: Team B may retain possession by declining the penalty for team A's motion foul. In that case, the penalty for team B's clipping foul will be enforced, yielding first and 10 for team B from team A's 45 yardline.

PLAY 5: First and 10 for team A from its own 20 yardline. A1's legal forward pass is intercepted by B2 at team A's 40 yardline. B2 advances to team A's 20 yardline. During B2's run, B3 is flagged for clipping at team A's 30 yardline and A4 grasps but does not twist B2's facemask at team A's 35 yardline. B2 fumbles and prone A5 recovers at team A's 35 yardline.

RULING 5: That is a double foul. Team A fouled before gaining final possession. The penalties cancel. It will be team A's ball, first and 10 at its own 20 yardline.

PLAYS INVOLVING THE END ZONE

Remember that while "team" designations (team A, team K, etc.) remain throughout a down, after a change of team possession, team A becomes the defense (the opponents of the team in possession) and team B becomes the offense (the team in possession.

CHAPTER 9

FOULS BY OPPONENTS OF THE TEAM IN POSSESSION

When the play results in a touchback, the basic spot is the 20 yardline. When the play results in a safety, the basic spot is the goalline.

PLAY 6: As seen in MechaniGram 9, B1 is at his own six yardline when he intercepts A2's legal forward pass. B1 runs into his own end zone, where he is downed. During B1's run, A3 grabs B4's facemask.

RULING 6: The play results in a safety because the team in possession is responsible for forcing the ball across its goalline. Team B will accept the penalty which is enforced from team B's goalline. It will be team B's ball, first and 10 from its own five yardline.

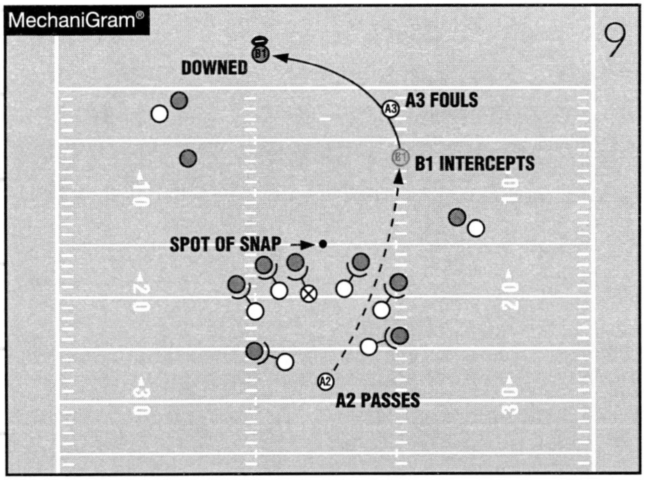

PLAY 7: B1 is in his own end zone when he intercepts A2's legal forward pass. B1 tries to advance but is downed without leaving the end zone. During B1's run, A3 grabs B4's facemask.

RULING 7: The play results in a touchback because the opponent of the team in possession is responsible for forcing the ball across the goalline of the team in possession. The penalty is enforced from the basic spot — team B's 20 yardline. It will be team B's ball, first and 10 from its own 25 yardline.

When, after a change of team possession, a related run ends in the end zone and either team fouls in the field of play, the basic spot is the 20 yardline.

PLAY 8: B1 is in his own end zone when he intercepts A2's legal forward pass. B1 tries to advance but is still in his end zone when he is hit and fumbles. The ball goes out of bounds. During B1's run, A3 grasps but does not twist B4's facemask at team B's 10 yardline.

RULING 8: The basic spot is team B's 20 yardline. The five-yard penalty is enforced from the basic spot. Team B will start a new series at its own 25 yardline.

The basic spot is the 20 yardline for fouls committed by either team when the opponent of the team in possession at the time of the foul is responsible for forcing the ball across the goalline of the team in possession and the related run ends in the end zone and is followed by a loose ball.

PLAY 9: B1 is in his own end zone when he intercepts A2's legal forward pass. B1 tries to advance but is still in his end zone when he is hit and fumbles. The ball goes out of bounds. During B1's run, A3 grasps but does not twist B4's facemask in the end zone.

RULING 9: The basic spot is the 20 yardline.

CHAPTER 9

The five-yard penalty is enforced from the basic spot, yielding first and 10 for team B from its own 25 yardline.

FOULS BY THE TEAM IN POSSESSION

Fouls by the team in possession after a change of possession are enforced using the all-but-one principle.

PLAY 10: B1 is in his own end zone when he intercepts A2's legal forward pass. B1 tries to advance but is downed without leaving the end zone. During B1's run, B3 clips A4 in the end zone.

RULING 10: Safety. The result of the play is a touchback because the opponent of the team in possession is responsible for forcing the ball across the goalline of the team in possession. Acceptance of the penalty results in a safety because the enforcement spot is in the end zone.

PLAY 11: B1 intercepts A2's legal forward pass at his own six yardline. B1 retreats to his own end zone and is downed there. During B1's run, B3 clips A4 in the end zone.

RULING 11: Safety. The result of the play is a safety because the team in possession is responsible for forcing the ball across its goalline. Acceptance of the penalty also results in a safety because the enforcement spot is in the end zone.

PLAY 12: As seen in MechaniGram 10, B1 is at his own six yardline when he intercepts A2's legal forward pass. B1 advances to his own 10 yardline, where he is downed. During B1's run, B3 clips A4 in the end zone.

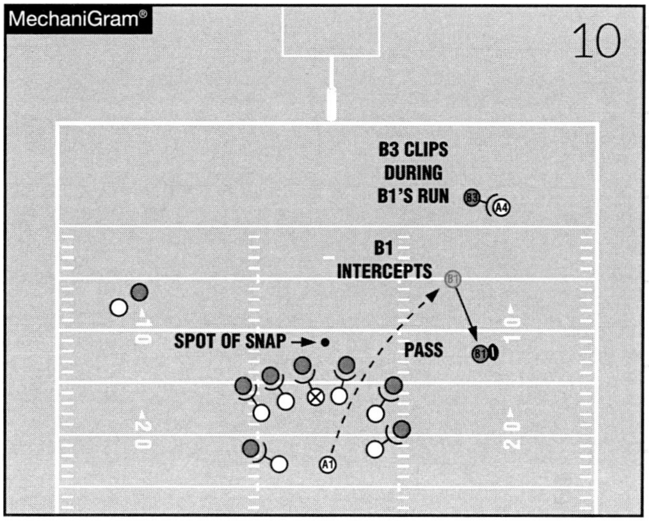

RULING 12: Safety. The result of the play is neither a safety nor a touchback — the ball became dead in the field of play. Acceptance of the penalty results in a safety because the enforcement spot is in the end zone.

If both the foul and the dead-ball spot are in the field of play, the penalty is enforced using the all-but-one principle.

PLAY 13: B1 is in his own end zone when he intercepts A2's legal forward pass. B1 advances to his own 15 yardline. During B1's run, (a) B3 clips A4 at team B's 10 yardline, or (b) A3 grabs B4's facemask at team B's 10 yardline.

RULING 13: The result of the play is neither a safety nor a touchback — the ball became dead in the field of play. The penalty is enforced using the all-but-one principle. In (a), the penalty is by the team in possession and is enforced from the spot of the foul. It will be team B's ball, first and 10 at its five yardline. In (b), the penalty is by the opponents of the team in possession and is enforced from the end of the run. It will be team B's ball, first and 10 at its 20 yardline.

When, after a change of team possession, a related run ends in the end zone and either team fouls in the field of play, the basic spot is the 20 yardline.

PLAY 14: As seen in MechaniGram 11, B1 is in his own end zone when he intercepts A2's legal forward pass. B1 tries to advance but is still in his end zone when he is hit and fumbles. The ball goes out of bounds. During B1's run, B3 clips A4 at team B's 14 yardline.

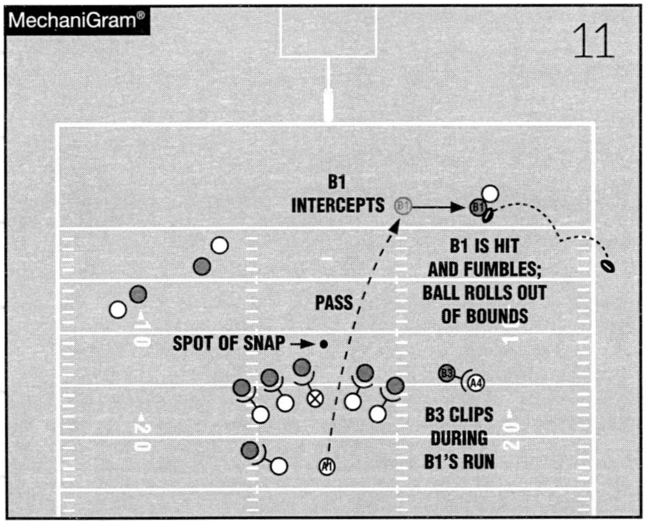

RULING 14: The basic spot is team B's 20 yardline. Because the foul occurred behind the basic spot, all-but-one enforcement applies. The penalty is enforced half the distance from team B's 14 yardline and yields first and 10 for team B from its own seven yardline.

When, after a change of team possession, a related run ends in the end zone and either team fouls in the end zone, the basic spot is the goalline.

FOULS ON CHANGE OF POSSESSION PLAYS

PLAY 15: B1 is in his own end zone when he intercepts A2's legal forward pass. B1 tries to advance but is still in his end zone when he is hit and fumbles. The ball goes out of bounds. During B1's run, B3 clips A4 in the end zone.

RULING 15: Safety. The basic spot is the goalline. The foul occurred behind the basic spot. Because the spot of the foul is in team B's end zone, the result is a safety.

Ordinarily, the momentum exception rewards a team for making a great play inside its own five yardline. However, the all-but-one principle still applies and can negate that stellar effort.

PLAY 16: B1 intercepts A2's legal forward pass at his own four yardline and his momentum takes him into his own end zone. B1 tries to advance but is still in his end zone when he is downed. During B1's run, B3 clips A4 in the end zone.

RULING 16: Safety. The basic spot is the momentum spot, team B's four yardline. The foul occurred behind the basic spot. Because the spot of the foul is in team B's end zone, the result is a safety.

CHAPTER 10

FOULS ON SCRIMMAGE-KICK PLAYS

FOULS ON SCRIMMAGE-KICK PLAYS

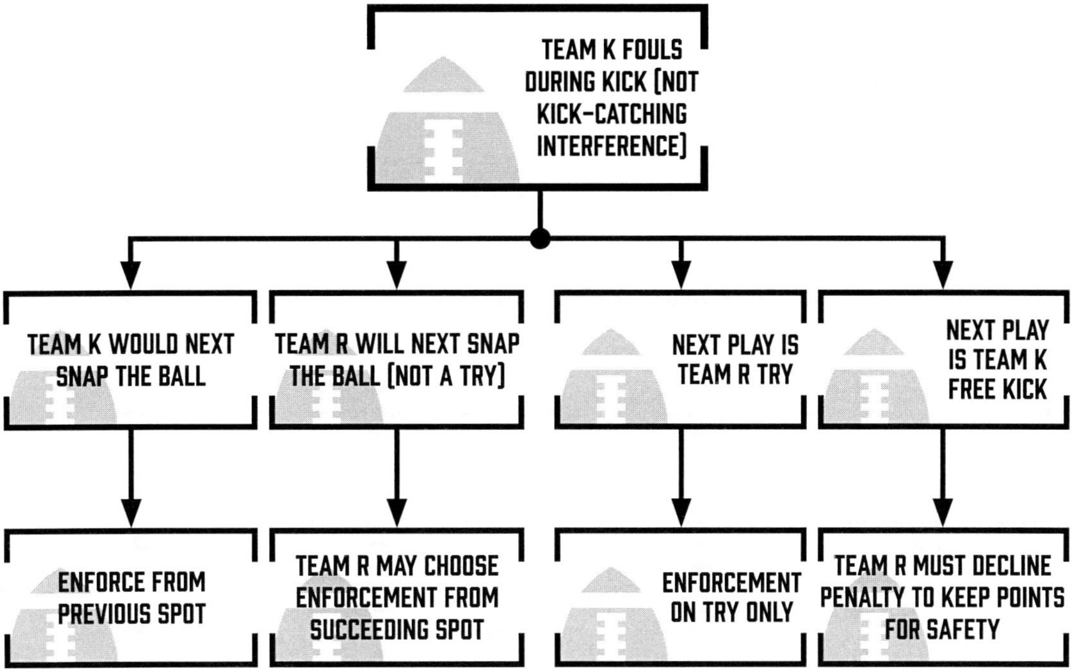

NOTE 1: Team R options on kick-catching interference:

- *Accept the results of the play*
- *Accept an awarded fair catch after enforcement of a 15-yard penalty from the spot of the foul*
- *Accept a 15-yard penalty from the previous spot and a replay of the down*

NOTE 2: Safety if team K fouls in its own end zone

FOULS ON SCRIMMAGE-KICK PLAYS

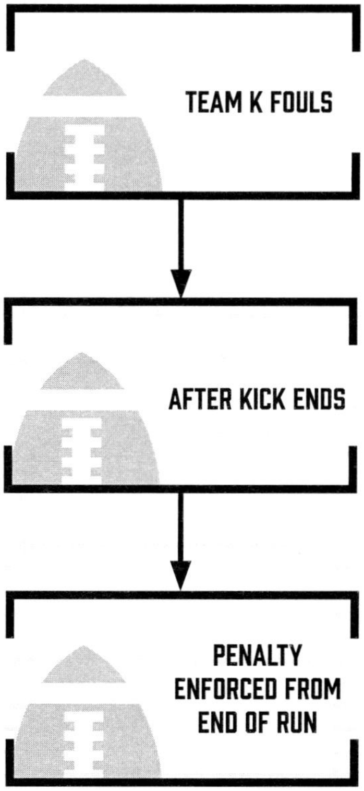

FOULS ON SCRIMMAGE-KICK PLAYS

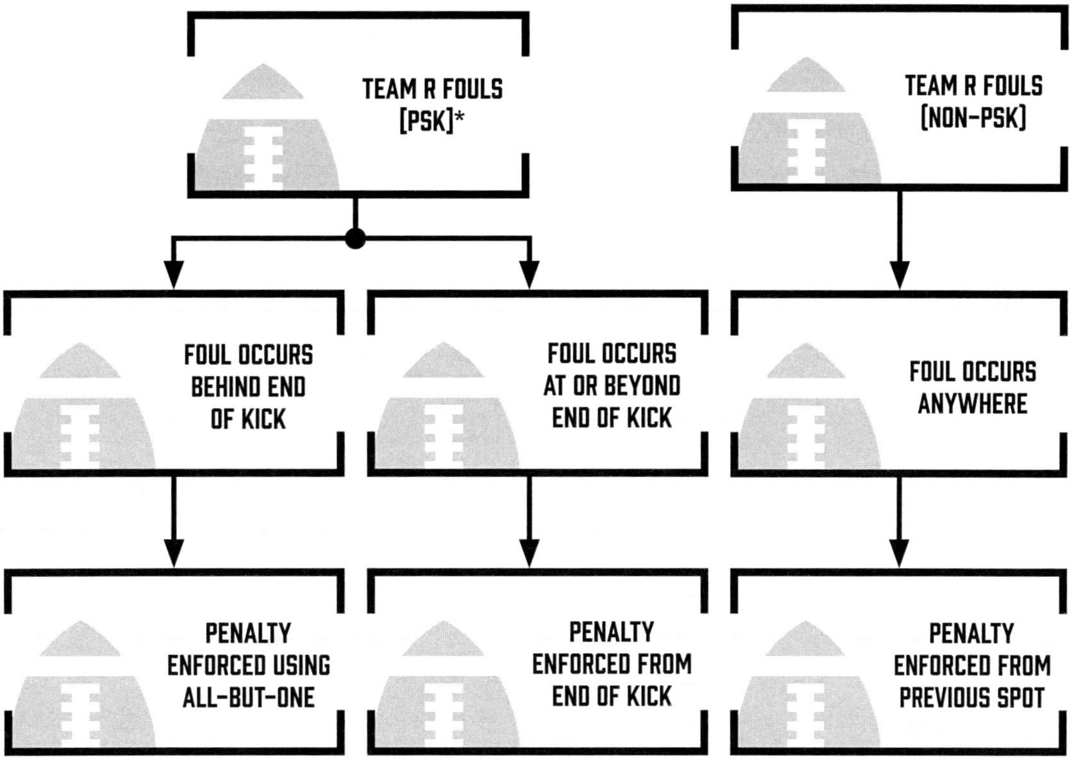

**PSK applies if team R fouls on team R's side of the expanded neutral zone prior to end of a scrimmage kick (other than a try or successful field goal) that crosses the neutral zone, if team K does not have possession of the ball when the down ends.*

CHAPTER 10

If team K commits a foul other than kick-catching interference during a scrimmage kick (from the time of the snap until the kick ends) and team K is not next to put the ball in play, team R has the option of enforcement from the succeeding spot. That is what is known as a "tack-on" penalty.

PLAY 1: Fourth and 10 from team K's 20 yardline. At the snap, team K is flagged for an illegal formation. K1's punt (a) is caught by R2 at the 50 yardline and returned to team K's 40 yardline, or (b) rolls untouched into team R's end zone.

RULING 1: In (a), team K may have the five-yard penalty enforced from the previous spot, or have the penalty enforced from the end of R2's run. In (b), because the result of the play is a touchback and the basic spot is team R's 20 yardline, enforcement from the succeeding spot would give team R a new series at its own 25 yardline.

PLAY 2: Fourth and 10 from team K's 20 yardline. As the kick is in flight, team K is flagged for an incidental grasp of a facemask. K1's punt is caught by R2 at the 50 yardline and returned to team K's 40 yardline, where R2 is hit and fumbles. The ball is recovered at team K's 35 yardline by (a) R3, or (b) K4.

RULING 2: In (a), the penalty is enforced from the end of the play. That gives team R a first down at team K's 30 yardline. In (b), in order to negate the loss of possession, team R must accept enforcement from the previous spot.

If team K fouls in its own end zone, acceptance of the penalty results in a safety. Team R may decline the penalty and keep the two points, or accept the penalty with previous spot enforcement. If team R scores a safety through play, the penalty may not be enforced because team K will next put the ball in play.

If team R scores a touchdown, the penalty may only be enforced on the try.

PLAY 3: Fourth and 10 from team K's five yardline. At the snap, team K is flagged for an illegal formation. K1's punt is blocked. The ball is recovered in team K's end zone by (a) R2, or (b) K3.

RULING 3: In (a), team R scores a touchdown. The five-yard penalty will be enforced on the try. There is no enforcement provision for giving the scoring team an option to enforce a penalty on the succeeding kickoff on a change-of-possession play when the foul occurs before the change of possession. In (b), team R scores a safety. The penalty cannot be enforced. Play resumes with team K's free kick from its own 20 yardline.

POST-SCRIMMAGE KICK ENFORCEMENT

Most fouls by team R during the kick play qualify for post-scrimmage kick (PSK) enforcement. PSK applies if team R fouls on team R's side of the expanded neutral zone prior to the end of a scrimmage kick (other than a try or successful field goal) that crosses the neutral zone, if team K does not have possession of the ball when the down ends.

If PSK does not apply, team R fouls before the kick ends have previous spot enforcement.

PLAY 4: Fourth and three on the 50 yardline. R1 gives an invalid fair-catch signal at his 20 yardline while the punt is in flight. R1 then catches the kick at his 15 yardline.

RULING 4: Team K would likely accept the five-yard penalty, which is assessed from the PSK spot (team R's 15 yardline) and results in team R's ball, first and 10 on team R's 10 yardline.

PLAY 5: As seen in MechaniGram 12, it's fourth and 10 for team K from team R's 40 yardline. While K1's punt is in flight, R2 blocks K3 below the waist. The foul occurs at team R's 18 yardline. The untouched kick lands in team R's end zone.

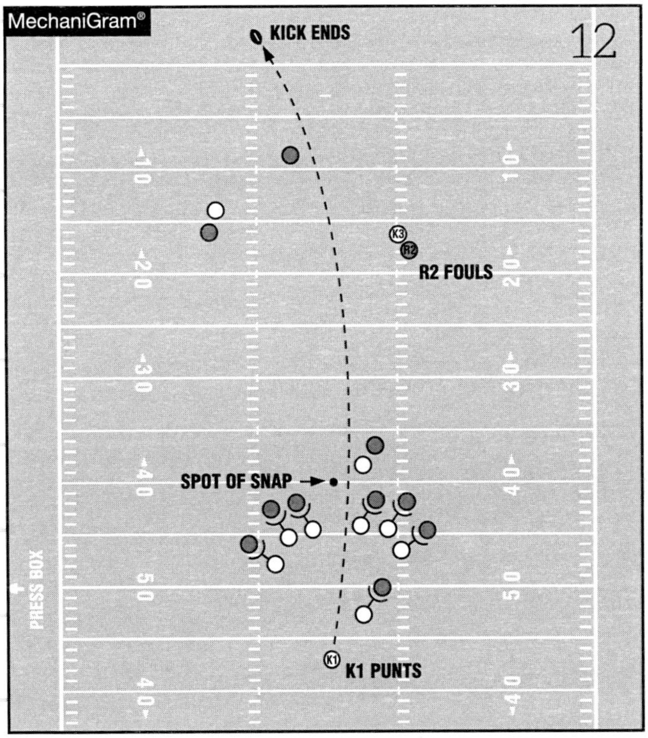

RULING 5: PSK applies. Because the kick resulted in a touchback, team R's 20 yardline is the basic spot. Because the spot of the foul is behind the basic spot, that is the spot of enforcement. It will be team R's ball, first and 10 from its own nine yardline.

PLAY 6: Fourth and 10 for team K from its own 20 yardline. While K1's punt is in flight, R2 blocks K3 below the waist. The foul occurs at team K's (a) 18, or (b) 23 yardline. R4 makes a fair catch at the 50 yardline.

RULING 6: R2's block is illegal and occurred before the kick ended. In (a), because the spot of the foul is behind the expanded neutral zone, PSK does not apply. The penalty is marked off 15 yards from the previous spot. That gives team K a new series at its own 35 yardline. In (b), PSK applies. The penalty is enforced from the end of the kick. It will be team R's ball, first and 10 at its own 35 yardline.

If PSK applies and the kick results in a touchback, team R's 20 yardline is the basic spot.

PLAY 7: Fourth and 10 for team K from its own 20 yardline. K1's punt is caught by R2 at team K's 45 yardline and he advances to team K's 35 yardline. During R2's run, a foul occurs at team K's 30 yardline. The foul is (a) clipping by R3, or (b) grasping and twisting the facemask by K4.

RULING 7: The fouls occurred during a running play. In (a), the penalty is enforced from the end of the run. It will be team R's ball, first and 10 at the 50 yardline. In (b), the penalty is added to the end of the run. It will be team R's ball, first and 10 at team K's 20 yardline.

PLAY 8: It is fourth and 10 for team K from its own 20 yardline. While K1's punt is in flight, R2 blocks K3 below the waist at the 50 yardline. R4 muffs the ball at team R's 45 yardline, where prone K5 recovers.

RULING 8: R2's block is illegal and occurred before the kick ended. However, PSK does not apply because team K was in possession at the end of the down. Team K will decline the penalty and start a new series, first and 10 at team R's 45 yardline.

CHAPTER 10

Live-ball fouls that occur after the kick ends are simply fouls during a running play.

PSK does not apply on a kick try or successful field goal. On successful scoring kicks, team K may have the penalty for team R fouls enforced from the previous spot or the succeeding spot. Team R fouls during an unsuccessful field goal are enforced under PSK or from the previous spot, depending on which applies.

PLAY 9: Fourth and 10 for team K from team R's 25 yardline. K1's attempted field goal is short, but R2 is flagged for grasping but not twisting K3's facemask at team R's 10 yardline. The untouched kick (a) lands in team R's end zone, or (b) comes to rest on team R's four yardline.

RULING 9: PSK applies in both cases. In (a), the result of the play is a touchback and the basic spot is team R's 20 yardline. The five-yard penalty is enforced from the spot of the foul because that is behind the PSK spot. That will leave team R with first and 10 from its own five yardline. In (b), the basic spot is the end of the kick, team R's four yardline. Because the foul occurred beyond the basic spot, the penalty is enforced from the basic spot, yielding first and 10 for team R from its own two yardline.

PLAY 10: Due to a penalty, team K is attempting a try from team R's 18 yardline. K1's attempted kick try is short, but R2 is flagged for grasping but not twisting K3's facemask at team R's 10 yardline. The untouched kick (a) lands in team R's end zone, or (b) comes to rest on team R's four yardline.

RULING 10: PSK does not apply on tries. If team K

accepts the penalty in (a) or (b), enforcement is from the previous spot. Team K will next snap the ball from team R's 13 yardline.

FIRST TOUCHING

First touching can add a confusing twist to penalty enforcement on scrimmage kicks. However, it is not difficult once you understand the fundamentals of first touching.

First touching is not a foul but has many of the same characteristics as a foul. It occurs when a team K player touches a scrimmage kick that has crossed the neutral zone before the ball is touched by a team R player. First touching gives team R the privilege of taking the ball at that spot of the touching. There cannot be first touching by team K in team R's end zone because the ball is dead once it breaks the plane of team R's goalline.

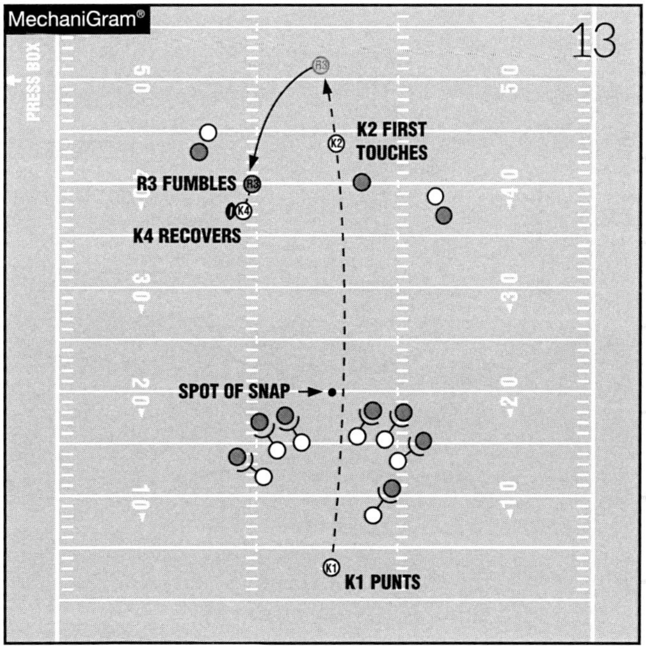

If team R touches the kick and thereafter during the down commits a foul, or if a penalty incurred by either team during the down is accepted, first touching privileges are cancelled.

PLAY 11: As seen in MechaniGram 13, it is fourth and 10 for team K from its own 20 yardline. K1's punt is first touched by K2 at team K's 45 yardline. R3 recovers the loose ball, advances to team K's 40 yardline and fumbles. Prone K4 recovers at team K's 37 yardline.

RULING 11: Team R will choose the spot of first touching rather than the result of the play. Team R will begin a new series at team K's 45 yardline.

PLAY 12: Fourth and 10 for team K from its own 20 yardline. K1's punt is first touched by K2 at team K's 45 yardline. R3 recovers the loose ball, advances to team K's 40 yardline and fumbles. K4 recovers and advances to the 50 yardline. During K4's run, K5 is flagged for holding at team K's 30 yardline.

RULING 12: If team R declines the penalty, it will take the ball at the spot of first touching (team K's 45 yardline). Accepting the penalty negates team R's ability to take the ball at the spot of first touching. However, it will force team K to start its new series at its own 20 yardline.

If each team fouls during a down in which there is a change of possession and all team R fouls have PSK enforcement, team R may retain the ball. In order for that to happen, team R must decline the penalty for team K fouls (other than nonplayer or unsportsmanlike).

PLAY 13: Fourth and 10 for team K from its own 20 yardline. Team K is illegally in motion at the snap. While the kick is in flight, R1 clips K2 at team K's 35 yardline. R3 makes a fair catch at team K's 40 yardline.

RULING 13: Team R may retain possession by declining the penalty for team K's motion foul. The penalty for R1's clip must be enforced. It will be team R's ball, first and 10 at its own 45 yardline.

FOULS ON SCRIMMAGE-KICK PLAYS

PLAY 14: As seen in MechaniGram 14, R1 catches a punt at his own four yardline. He advances to his own 15 yardline, where he is downed. During the run, R2 clips K3 in team R's end zone.

RULING 14: Safety. Team R's foul is behind the end of the run and is in team R's end zone.

PLAY 15: K1's untouched punt rolls into team R's end zone. While the ball is in flight, R2 clips K3. The foul occurs (a) in team R's end zone, (b) at team R's six yardline, or (c) team R's 24 yardline.

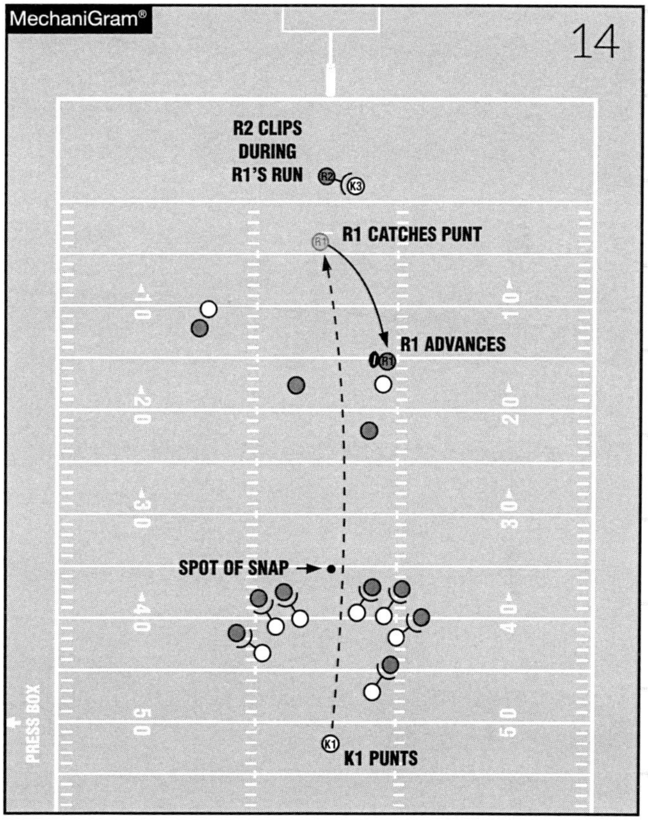

RULING 15: In all three cases, the play results in a touchback and the basic spot is team R's 20 yardline. In (a), team K scores a safety because the spot of the foul is behind the basic spot and the foul occurs in team R's end zone. In (b), the foul occurs behind the basic spot. The penalty is enforced from the spot of the foul. The result is first and 10 from team R's three yardline. In (c), the foul occurred beyond the basic spot. The penalty is enforced from the basic spot, yielding first and 10 for team R from its 10 yardline.

CHAPTER 11

DEAD-BALL FOULS

DEAD-BALL FOULS

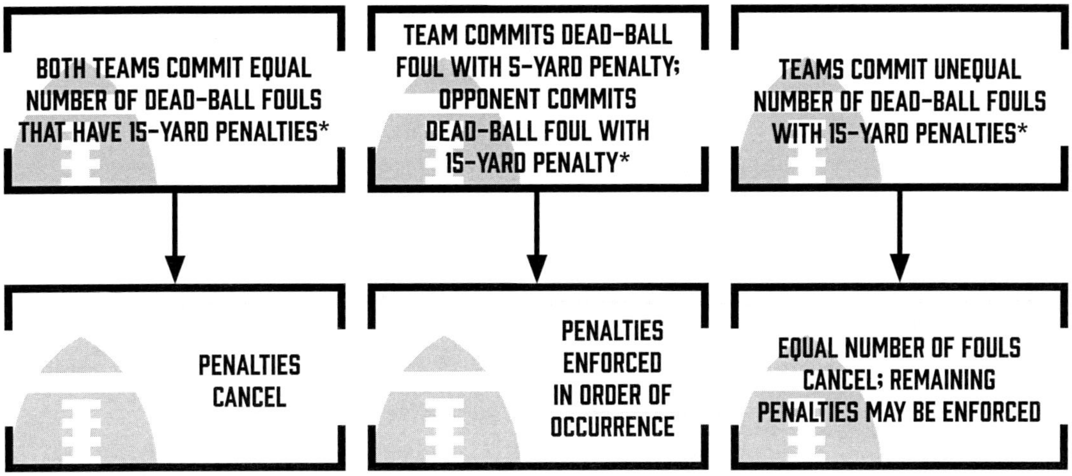

*Includes live-ball fouls enforced as dead-ball fouls

CHAPTER 11

Dead-ball fouls are fouls that occur from the time the ball is dead until it is next snapped or free kicked.

The distance penalty for unsportsmanlike, nonplayer or dead-ball personal fouls committed by teams can offset. Equal numbers of 15-yard penalties by both teams will cancel and remaining penalties may be enforced.

If both teams commit unsportsmanlike, nonplayer or dead-ball personal fouls prior to the completion of penalty administration for those fouls, the distance penalty for an equal number of 15-yard unsportsmanlike, nonplayer or dead-ball personal fouls will offset. Any remaining penalties will be enforced separately and in the order of occurrence.

The "trigger" for determining when penalty administration is completed is the referee signaling the foul.

Dead-ball fouls are enforced from the succeeding spot and the down counts.

Unsportsmanlike conduct and nonplayer fouls occurring while the ball is live are considered live-ball fouls enforced as dead-ball fouls. That includes the situation in which an official makes accidental contact with a nonplayer in the restricted area while the ball is live. There is no "spot" of the foul in those circumstances. Those fouls are enforced at the end of the play.

Live-ball fouls enforced as dead-ball fouls do not combine with another live-ball foul to create a double or multiple foul.

A dead-ball foul is not coupled with a live-ball foul or another dead-ball foul to create a double or multiple foul.

For enforcement of unsportsmanlike and dead-ball fouls involving scoring plays, see Chapter 15.

Equal numbers of 15-yard penalties by both teams will cancel and remaining penalties may be enforced.

PLAY 1: B2 is flagged for a late hit on A1. A1 responds by cursing at B2.

RULING 1: Both fouls are treated as dead-ball fouls. The penalties cancel.

PLAY 2: B2 is flagged for a late hit on A1. A1 responds by cursing at B2. B3 curses at A1.

RULING 2: All fouls are treated as dead-ball fouls. The penalties for A1's and B2's fouls cancel. The penalty for B3's foul is enforced from the succeeding spot.

PLAY 3: Third and 20 at team A's 25 yardline. A1 false starts. B2 reacts by crossing the neutral zone and forcibly contacting A1.

RULING 3: Only fouls that have a 15-yard penalty cancel. The penalties are enforced in the order of occurrence. The penalty for A1's foul is enforced to team A's 20 yardline, then the penalty for B2's personal foul is enforced. The result is third and 10 for team A from its own 35 yardline.

PLAY 3: B2 is flagged for a late hit. Before the penalty is enforced, B2 curses the official.

RULING 3: The penalties for both of B2's fouls will be enforced from the succeeding spot.

FOULS THAT PREVENT THE SNAP

Fouls that prevent the snap include delay of game, an illegal snap, false start and encroachment. Penalties for those fouls are enforced from the succeeding spot and the down remains the same.

CHAPTER 12

LIVE-BALL FOLLOWED BY DEAD-BALL FOULS

LIVE-BALL FOLLOWED BY DEAD-BALL FOULS

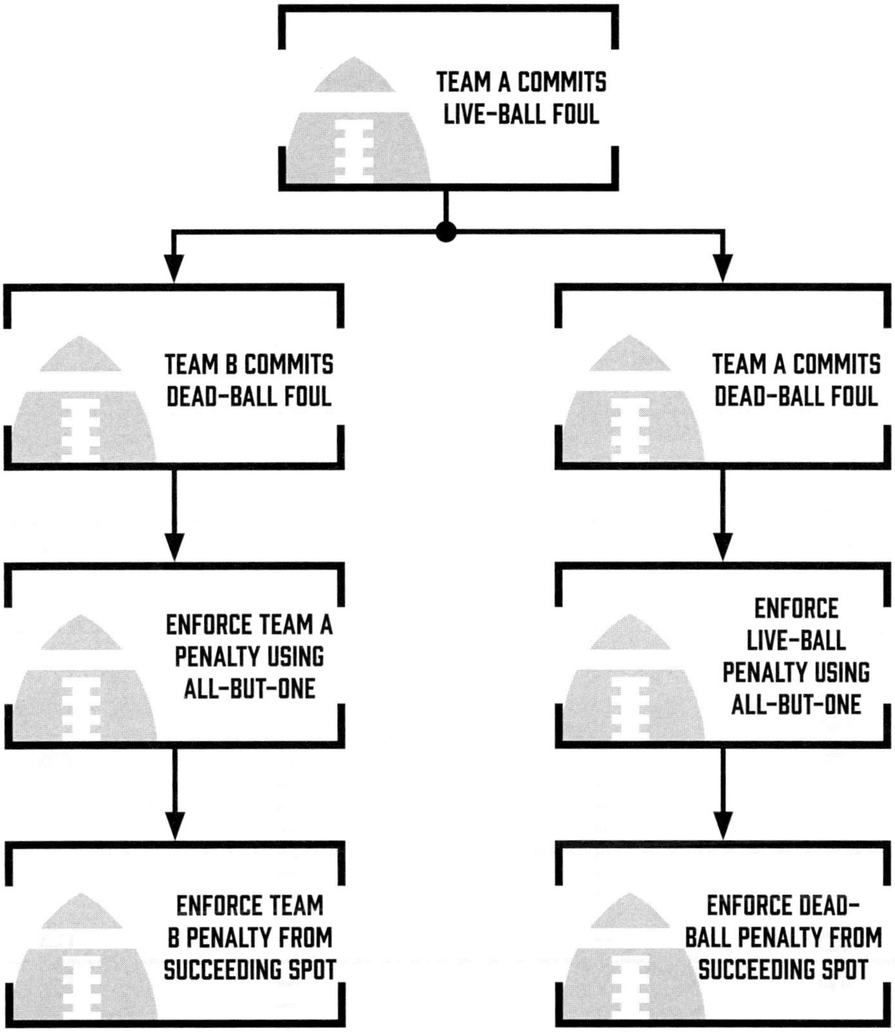

LIVE-BALL FOLLOWED BY DEAD-BALL FOULS

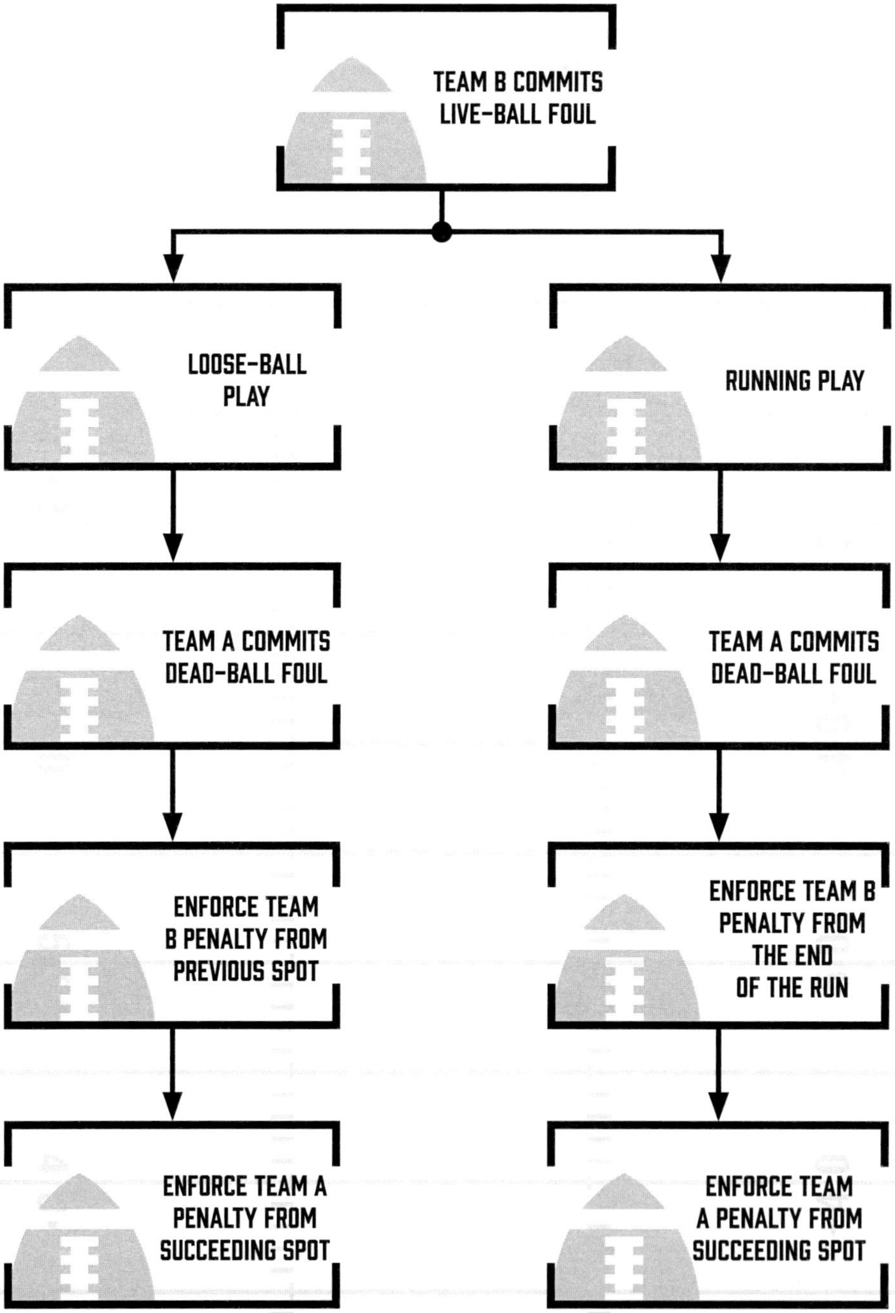

LIVE-BALL FOLLOWED BY DEAD-BALL FOULS

If one team commits a live-ball foul followed by a dead-ball foul (or a live-ball foul enforced as a dead-ball foul), the fouls are enforced separately and in the order of their occurrence.

PLAY 1: As seen in MechaniGram 15, it's first and 10 for team A from team B's 15 yardline. Team A is flagged for illegal motion at the snap. A1 breaks into the clear and is running for an apparent touchdown. At team B's five yardline, he turns and taunts the team B players chasing him.

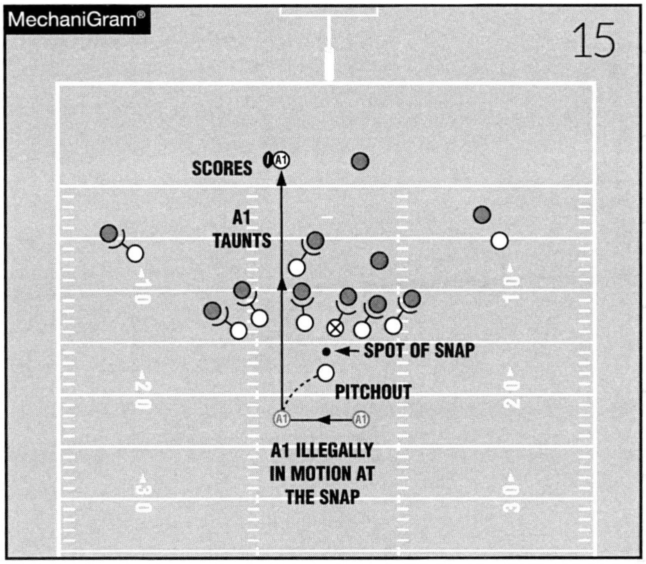

RULING 1: Team B will likely accept both penalties. The motion penalty moves the ball back to team B's 20 yardline. The penalty for A1's unsportsmanlike act is enforced from that spot. It will be team A's ball, first and 30 at team B's 35 yardline.

PLAY 2: Fourth and 10 for team K from its own 18 yardline. Team K is flagged for illegal motion at the snap. R1 returns the punt to team K's 40 yardline. After the whistle sounds, R2 is flagged for a late hit at team K's 35 yardline.

RULING 2: Team R will decline the penalty for team K's motion foul. The penalty for R2's dead-ball foul is enforced from the succeeding spot. Team R will start a new series at its own 45 yardline.

The distance penalty for unsportsmanlike, nonplayer or dead-ball personal fouls committed by teams can offset. Equal numbers of 15-yard penalties by both teams will cancel and remaining penalties may be enforced.

CHAPTER 12

If one team commits a non-15-yard dead-ball foul and the other commits a 15-yard dead-ball foul, the penalties are enforced in the order of occurrence.

PLAY 3: First and 10 for team A from its own 10 yardline. A1 false starts. B2 charges across the line and roughly contacts A3.

RULING 3: Both are dead-ball fouls. The penalty for team A's foul takes the ball to team A's five yardline. The penalty for B2's personal foul is then enforced, yielding first and 10 for team A from its own 20 yardline.

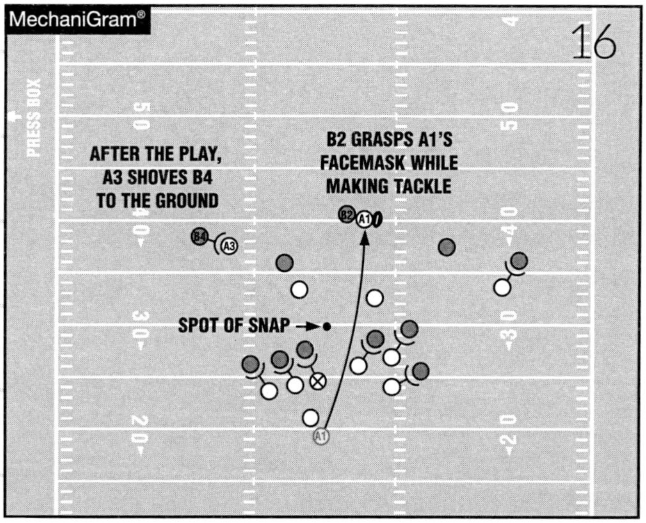

PLAY 4: First and 10 for team A from its own 10 yardline. A1's run gains four yards. After the ball is dead, A2 and B3 slug each other. The official flagging the incident (a) sees A2 punch first, followed by B3, or (b) does not know who threw the first punch.

RULING 4: In (a) or (b), the fouls offset. However, both players are disqualified for fighting.

PLAY 5: As seen in MechaniGram 16, it's second and five for team A from its own 30 yardline. A1's run gains 10 yards and B2 is flagged for grasping but not twisting A1's facemask. After the play has ended, A3 shoves B4 to the ground.

RULING 5: A live-ball foul cannot be coupled with a dead-ball foul to create a double foul. The penalty for B2's live-ball foul is administered, moving the ball to team A's 45 yardline (beyond the line to gain). The 15-yard penalty for the dead-ball foul is administered from that spot. It will be first and 10 for team A from its own 30 yardline.

PLAY 6: Fourth and 10 at team K's 40 yardline. R1 runs into punter K2. R3 fair-catches the punt at his own 30 yardline. K4 is flagged for a dead-ball personal foul.

RULING 6: If team K declines the penalty for running into the kicker, only the penalty for its dead-ball foul would be enforced. Team K's best option would be to accept the penalty for running into the kicker, which is enforced from the previous spot. The penalty for the dead-ball foul is then enforced from that spot. The result is a replay of the down, fourth and 20 from team K's 30 yardline.

PLAY 7: Fourth and 10 at team K's 40 yardline. R1 runs into punter K2. R3 fair-catches the punt at his own 30 yardline. R4 is flagged for a dead-ball personal foul.

RULING 7: Both penalties may be enforced from the previous spot. The result is first and 10 for team K from team R's 40 yardline.

PLAY 8: Third and 20 from team A's 30 yardline with three seconds left in the second quarter. At the snap, team A is flagged for an illegal shift. A1 is downed on his own 15 yardline as time expires. After the ball is dead, B2 commits an unsportsmanlike conduct foul.

RULING 8: If team B accepts the penalty for team A's foul, it moves the ball to team A's 25 yardline. Team A would then accept the penalty for the unsportsmanlike foul, which places the ball at team B's 40 yardline, where it will be third and 10. An untimed down would then be played. If team B declines the penalty, the half is over and the penalty for the unsportsmanlike foul will be assessed on the second-half kickoff.

CHAPTER 13

DOUBLE AND MULTIPLE FOULS

DOUBLE AND MULTIPLE FOULS

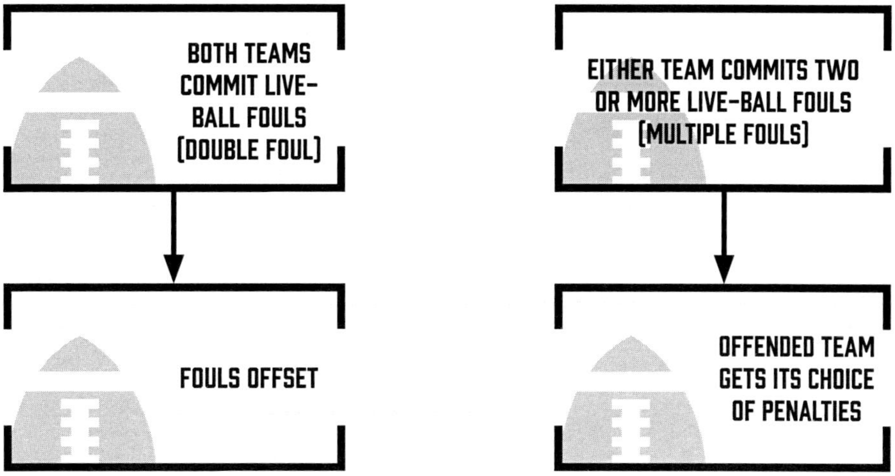

CHAPTER 13

DOUBLE FOULS

A double foul occurs when each team commits one or more live-ball fouls (other than nonplayer or unsportsmanlike) at such a time that the penalties offset.

If both teams foul and there is no change of possession, the fouls offset and the down is replayed.

PLAY 1: First and 10 for team A from its own 20 yardline. Team A is flagged for illegal motion at the snap. A1's legal forward pass results in a pass interference foul on B2.

RULING 1: That is a double foul. The penalties cancel and the down is replayed.

MULTIPLE FOULS

A multiple foul occurs when one team commits two or more live-ball fouls (other than nonplayer or unsportsmanlike). The offended team has its choice of which penalty to accept.

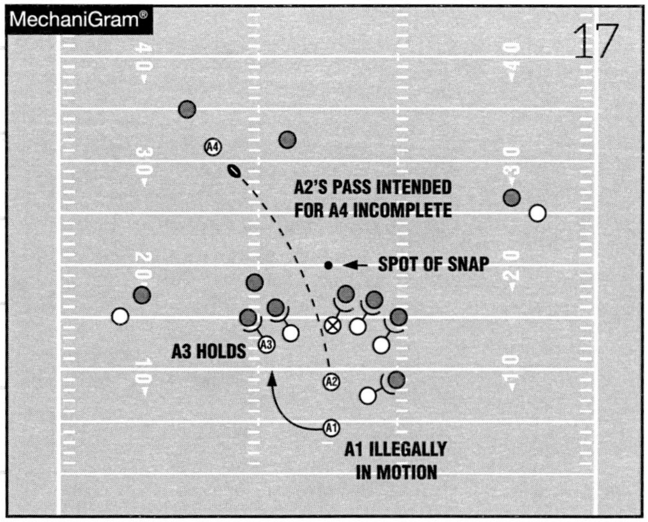

PLAY 2: As seen in MechaniGram 17, it's first and 10 for team A on its own 20 yardline. A1 is flagged for illegal motion at the snap. A2's legal forward pass is incomplete. While the pass is in flight, A3 is flagged for holding at team A's 16 yardline.

RULING 2: Team B will have its choice of penalties. It is likely the holding penalty will be enforced half the distance to the goal, leaving team A with first and 22 at its own eight yardline.

CHAPTER 14

DOUBLE AND MULTIPLE FOULS WITH CHANGE OF POSSESSION

DOUBLE AND MULTIPLE FOULS WITH CHANGE OF POSSESSION

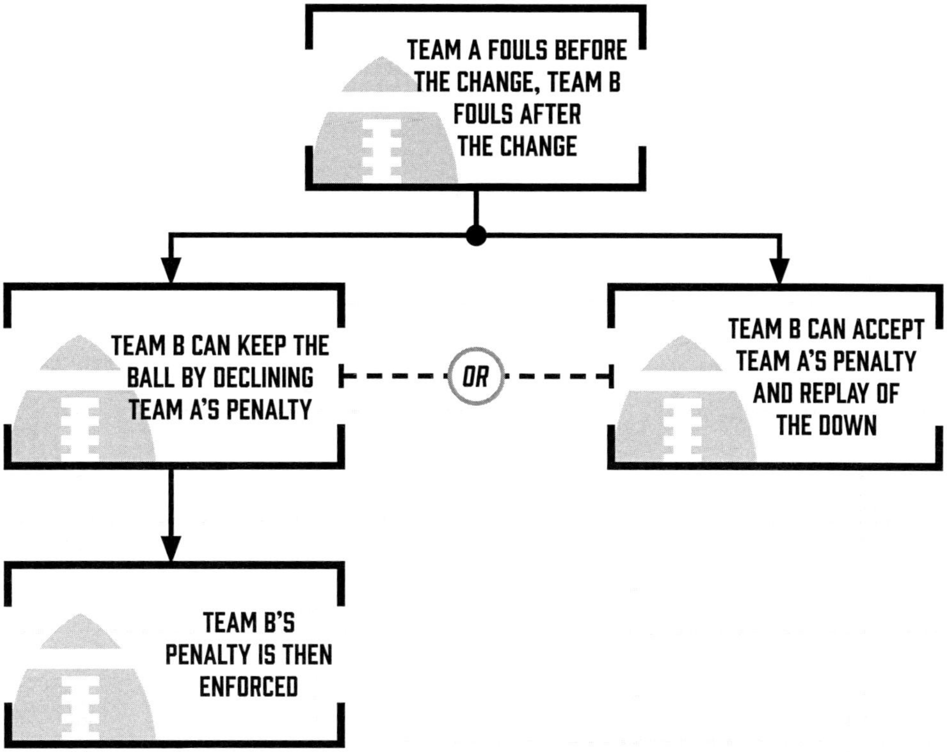

DOUBLE AND MULTIPLE FOULS WITH CHANGE OF POSSESSION

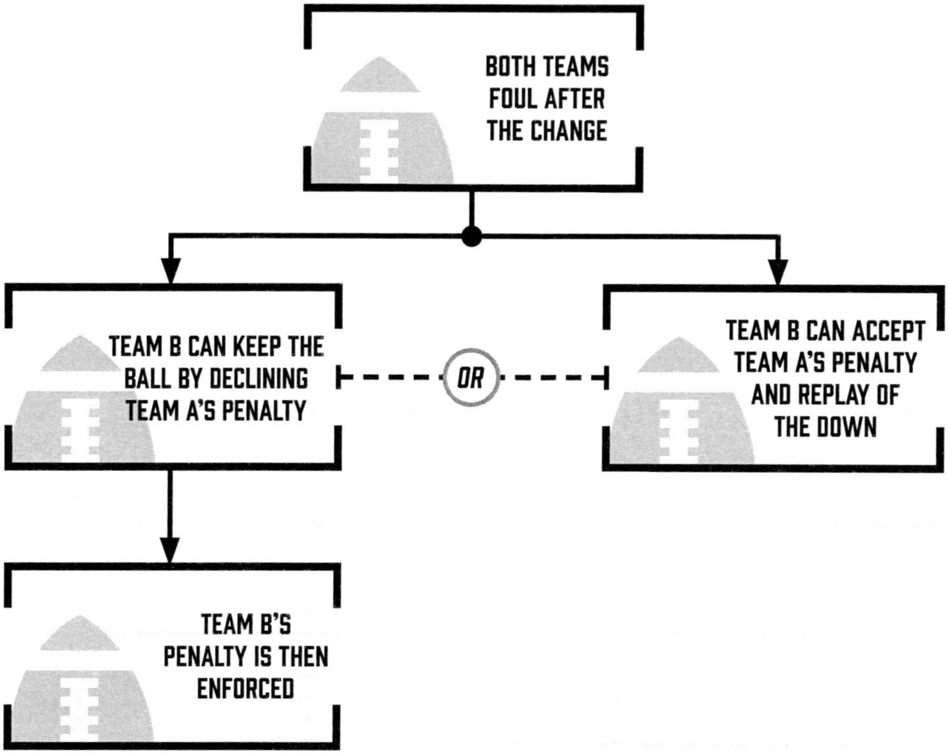

DOUBLE AND MULTIPLE FOULS WITH CHANGE OF POSSESSION

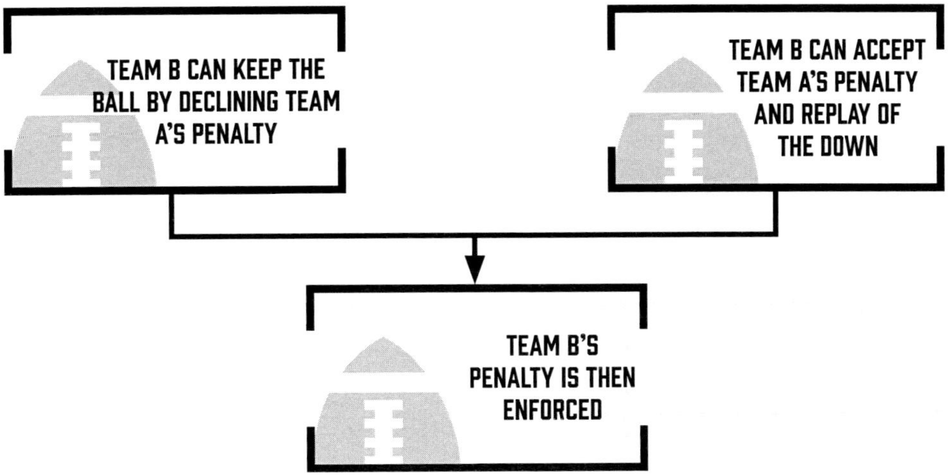

CHAPTER 14

If both teams foul before a change of possession, the down is replayed unless post-scrimmage kick enforcement applies. If team B fouls before the change and team A fouls before or after the change, the down is replayed because team B didn't get the ball with "clean hands."

If team A fouls before the change and team B fouls after the change, team B may keep the ball by declining team A's penalty. The penalty for team B's foul is then enforced; team A has no option. Team B can also take offsetting fouls and have the down replayed.

If team A's and team B's fouls occur after a change of possession, team B has the option of keeping the ball if it declines the penalty for team A's foul. The penalty for team B's foul is then enforced. Team B can also take offsetting fouls and have the down replayed.

PLAY 1: Team A is flagged for illegal motion at the snap. B1 intercepts at his own 10 yardline and advances to team B's 40 yardline. During B1's run, B2 clips at team B's 10 yardline.

RULING 1: Team B may keep the ball by declining the penalty for team A's foul. The penalty for team B's foul must then be enforced. The result is first and 10 for team B from its own five yardline. If team B accepts the penalty, it would result in a double foul and a replay of the down.

PLAY 2: B1 intercepts a pass at team B's 10 yardline and advances. During B1's run, B2 blocks below the waist at team B's 20 yardline. As A3 tackles B1 at team B's 40 yardline, A3 grasps but does not twist B1's facemask.

RULING 2: Team B can keep the ball by declining the penalty for team A's foul. The penalty for B2's foul would then be enforced from the spot of the foul. That would yield team B's ball, first and 10 at its own 10 yardline. If team B accepts the penalty for team A's foul, the fouls would offset and the down replayed.

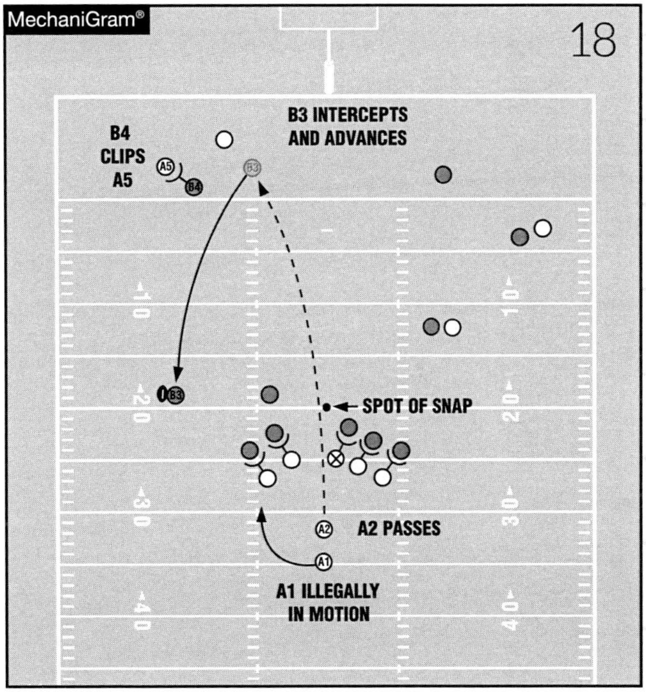

PLAY 3: As seen in MechaniGram 18, A1 is flagged for illegal motion at the snap. A2's legal forward pass is intercepted by B3 in his own end zone and returned to his own 20 yardline. During B2's run, B4 clips A5 in team B's end zone.

RULING 3: If team B declined team A's penalty, it would result in a safety. Team B will likely accept team A's penalty, resulting in a double foul and a replay of the down.

PLAY 4: Team A is flagged for illegal motion at the snap and team B is flagged for pass interference. The pass is intercepted.

RULING 4: Both fouls occurred in the first segment. The result is offsetting fouls and a replay.

If a team gains possession with clean hands and each team fouls after the change, the team in possession may keep the ball.

PLAY 5: As seen in MechaniGram 19, K1 kicks off from his own 40 yardline. While the ball is in flight, K2 grasps but does not twist R3's facemask at the 50 yardline and R4 holds K5 at team R's 40 yardline. R6 catches the kick at his own 15 yardline and is downed at team R's 20 yardline.

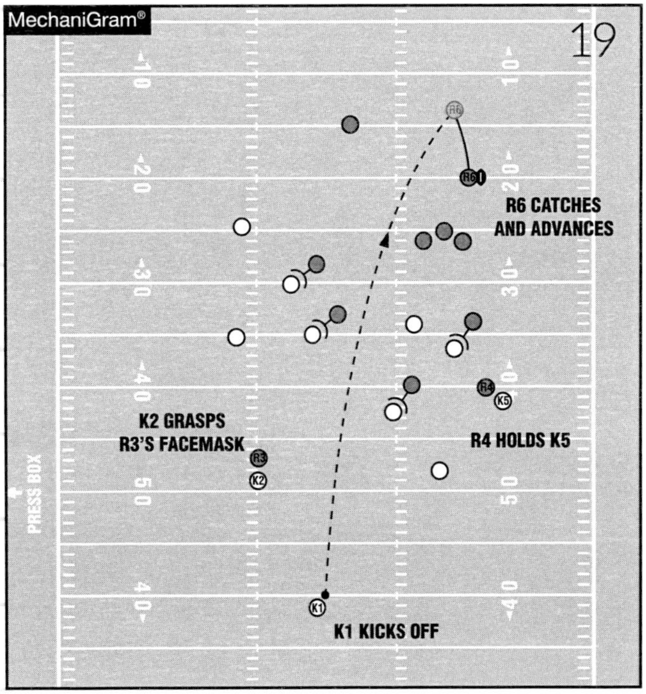

RULING 5: It is a double foul during a loose-ball play because both fouls occurred before the kick ended. The penalties cancel and the down is replayed.

Neither team can keep the ball if it did not get it with clean hands. Once a team commits a foul, its hands are "dirty" for the remainder of the down. Analyze each portion of the play as segments: the first segment is prior to the first change, the second segment is prior to the second change, the third segment is prior to the third change, etc.

DOUBLE AND MULTIPLE FOULS WITH CHANGE OF POSSESSION

If both teams foul in the first segment (before the change), the penalties cancel by rule and the down will be replayed because neither team got the ball with clean hands.

PLAY 6: Team A is flagged for illegal motion at the snap. B1 intercepts a legal forward pass and advances. During B1's run, B2 clips. A3 grasps but does not twist B1's facemask while making the tackle.

RULING 6: Since team B gained possession with clean hands and its foul occurred in the second segment, the foul in the first segment is declined and the fouls after the change are addressed. Team B can choose offsetting fouls and a replay of the down or decline the penalty for A3's foul and keep the ball after enforcement of the penalty for B2's foul.

If both teams foul during the down and there are two or more changes of possession during the down, it is called a "double foul/double change."

PLAY 7: Team A is flagged for illegal motion at the snap. B1 intercepts a legal forward pass and advances. During B1's run, B2 clips and A3 grasps but does not twist B1's facemask. B1 fumbles and team A recovers.

RULING 7: Team A gained possession with dirty hands. Because the team last gaining possession fouled before gaining final possession, the fouls offset and the down is replayed.

CHAPTER 15

CARRYOVER FOULS ("BRIDGES")

CARRYOVER FOULS ["BRIDGES"]

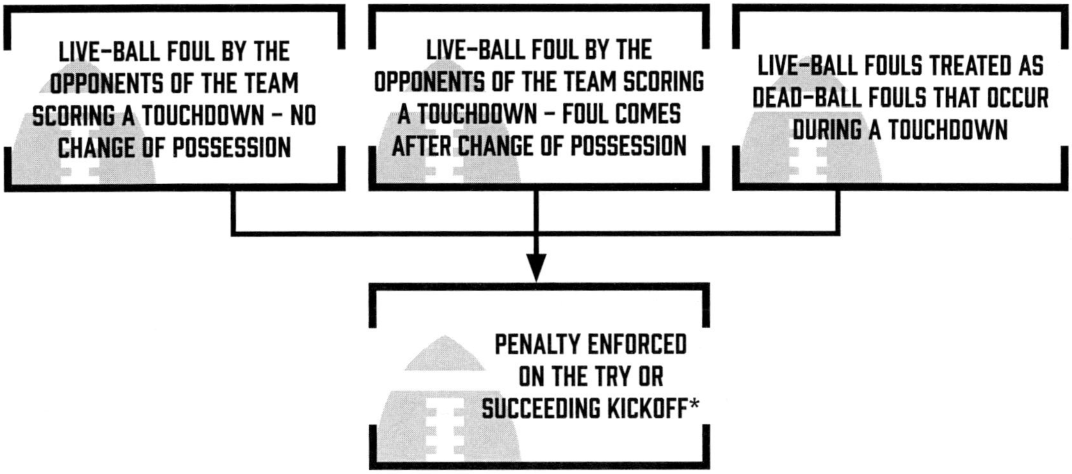

**If the foul occurs during the last timed down of the second quarter, the scoring team may choose enforcement on the try or the third-quarter kickoff.*

If the foul occurs during the last timed down of the fourth quarter, the scoring team MAY NOT choose enforcement in overtime (in the event a successful try would send the game to overtime). If the foul occurs during the last timed down of the fourth quarter and the try is not needed for playoff qualifying, the penalty is not enforced and the game ends. If the try is necessary, the penalty can only be enforced on the try.

CARRYOVER FOULS ["BRIDGES"]

FOUL BY THE OPPONENT OF THE SCORING TEAM ON A SUCCESSFUL KICK TRY OR FIELD GOAL

↓

OFFENDED TEAM MAY CHOOSE ENFORCEMENT FROM PREVIOUS SPOT AND REPLAY OF DOWN

OR

↓

ENFORCE ON ENSUING KICKOFF OR SUCCEEDING SPOT IN OVERTIME

CARRYOVER FOULS ["BRIDGES"]

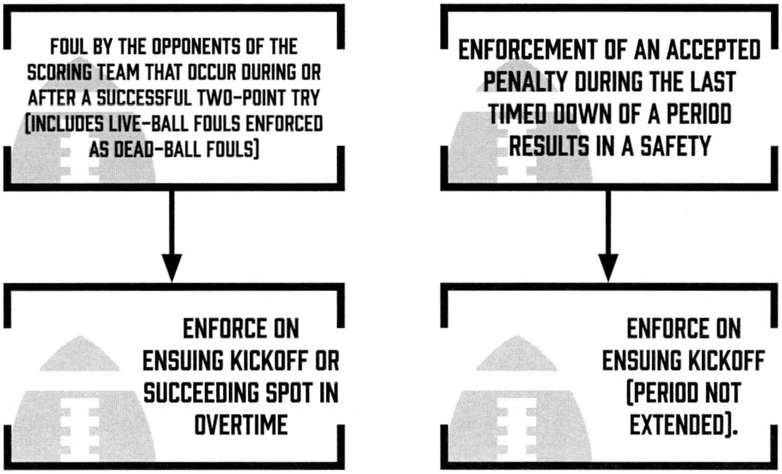

CHAPTER 15

Some penalties for fouls that occur during plays involving touchdowns can be "bridged" (carried over) from the try to the succeeding kickoff, from one period to the next and from the fourth quarter to the succeeding spot in overtime. Bridge is not a term used in the rulebook. It is used here to help officials understand the concept of carrying a penalty over.

The team scoring a touchdown may choose to have the penalty enforced on the ensuing free kick. (The offended team may still choose to have the penalty enforced on the try. See Chapter 16).

The option applies if team B commits a live-ball foul on a play on which team A scores a touchdown, or if team A commits a live-ball foul after a change of possession and team B scores. However, if the foul is by team A before the change of possession and team B gains possession and then scores, team B must decline team A's foul to keep the score.

Dead-ball fouls committed after the touchdown is scored but before the next ready signal, and unsportsmanlike conduct fouls occurring during or after the down, can be enforced on the try or can bridge to the kickoff. However, they may not bridge to overtime.

PLAY 1: A1's run from scrimmage results in a touchdown. During A1's run, B1 is flagged for (a) grasping but not twisting A1's facemask, or (b) cursing the official.

RULING 1: In (a) and (b), the touchdown counts. In either case, team A may choose to have the penalty enforced on the try, or choose to have the penalty bridge to the kickoff.

PLAY 2: A1's pass is intercepted by B1 and returned for a touchdown. A2 grasps but does not twist B1's facemask (a) before, or (b) after B1 intercepts.

RULING 2: In (a), the foul occurred before the change of possession. Team B must decline the penalty to keep the touchdown. In (b), because the foul occurred after the change, team B may choose enforcement on the try or on the ensuing kickoff.

PLAY 3: A1's pass from scrimmage results in a touchdown. B2 is flagged for roughing the passer. Team A's captain chooses to have the penalty enforced on the subsequent kickoff. On the try, B3 is flagged for roughing the kicker. The (a) kick try is successful, or (b) unsuccessful.

RULING 3: In (a), team A may choose to have the roughing the kicker penalty enforced from the previous spot and replay the try, or have the penalty enforced on the subsequent kickoff. If team A chooses the latter, it will kick off from team B's 30 yardline after both penalties are enforced. In (b), the penalty is enforced from the previous spot and the down is replayed.

PLAY 4: A1's run from scrimmage results in a touchdown. During A1's run, B1 grasps but does not twist A1's facemask. Team A chooses to have the five-yard penalty enforced on the succeeding kickoff. On the successful try, A2 is flagged for a (a) live-ball, or (b) dead-ball personal foul.

RULING 4: In (a), if team B wants to accept the penalty for the foul committed by A2, it must be enforced on the try. The down would be replayed with the ball being snapped from team B's 18 yardline. The penalty for B1's foul will still be enforced on the ensuing kickoff; team A is not allowed to reconsider its option. In (b), a live-ball foul on one team and a dead-ball foul on the other cannot result in a double foul. The penalties are enforced on the kickoff in the order of occurrence. The penalty for B1's foul moves the ball to team A's 45 yardline. The penalty for A2's foul moves the ball back to team A's 30 yardline, and team A will kick off from that spot.

Assuming no change of possession, the only team A fouls that may bridge to the kickoff or succeeding spot in overtime are dead-ball fouls or live-ball fouls treated as dead-ball fouls.

PLAY 5: With 4:37 to play in the first quarter, A1 taunts B2 on a play that results in a (a) touchdown, or (b) two-point try.

RULING 5: In (a), team B has the option of having the penalty enforced on the try or the subsequent kickoff. In (b), the penalty bridges to the kickoff.

LAST TIMED DOWN OF THE FIRST, SECOND OR THIRD QUARTER

If a bridge foul on a score occurs during the last timed down of the first, second or third quarter and the team elects to have the penalty enforced on the kickoff, the period is extended for the try only, not the kickoff. The kickoff is the first play of the next quarter.

PLAY 6: Team A scores a touchdown during the last timed down of the second quarter. Team A's attempted two-point try is successful and B1 is flagged for roughing the passer.

RULING 6: If team A accepts the penalty, it will be enforced from the succeeding spot, which will be the kickoff to begin the third quarter. Note that if the touchdown were scored during the last timed down of the first or third quarters, the kickoff would occur after the teams change ends for the second or fourth quarter.

PLAY 7: Team A scores a touchdown during the last timed down of the second quarter. During the play, B1 is flagged for grasping but not twisting A1's facemask.

RULING 7: Team A may choose to have the penalty enforced on the try as an untimed down and an extension of the second quarter, or from the succeeding spot, which will be the kickoff to begin the third quarter. Note that if the touchdown were scored during the last timed down of the first or third quarters, the kickoff would occur after the teams change ends for the second or fourth quarter.

If the opponent of the scoring team fouls during the touchdown-scoring play and the scoring team chooses enforcement on the next kickoff, then the same team commits a live-ball foul on the try, the scoring team may choose to have both penalties enforced on the next kickoff.

PLAY 8: In the middle of the third quarter, A1's run from scrimmage results in a touchdown. During A1's run, B1 is flagged for grasping but not twisting A1's facemask. Team A's captain chooses to have the penalty enforced on the subsequent kickoff. During the successful try, B2 is flagged for roughing the kicker.

RULING 8: Team A may choose to have the roughing penalty enforced from the previous spot and replay the try, or have the penalty enforced on the subsequent kickoff. If team A chooses the latter, it will kick off from team B's 40 yardline.

If, during the last timed down of a period, enforcement of an accepted penalty results in a safety, the period is not extended for the ensuing kickoff. The teams change goals and the free kick is the first play of the next quarter.

CHAPTER 15

PLAY 9: First and 10 for team A from its own three yardline. A1 drops back into his own end zone, which is on the north end of the field. A flag is thrown for (a) A2's holding foul in the end zone on A1's incomplete pass, (b) A1's illegal forward pass from the end zone, or (c) B3's roughing the passer on A1's incomplete pass. Time for the first or third quarter expires during the down.

RULING 9: In (a) and (b), if team B accepts the penalty, the result is a safety. Team B scores two points and the second or fourth period begins with team A's free kick from the 20 yardline at the south end of the field. In (c), if team A accepts the penalty, it is enforced 15 yards from the previous spot and includes an automatic first down. The period is extended for an untimed down.

LAST TIMED DOWN OF FOURTH QUARTER

It is not possible for the scoring team to bridge to the overtime a penalty for a live-ball foul that occurs during a touchdown during the last timed down of the fourth quarter. It is possible for the scoring team to bridge to the overtime a penalty for a live-ball foul by the opponent that occurs during a field goal or try during the last timed down of the fourth quarter.

PLAY 10: Team A trails by seven points late in the game. A1's run results in a touchdown as time runs out. During A1's run, B1 is flagged for grasping but not twisting A1's facemask. Thinking it can tie the game with a kick and send the game to overtime, team A wants to delay enforcement to the succeeding spot in overtime.

RULING 10: That is not allowed. The additional enforcement option carries over to the next kickoff, not the succeeding spot in overtime. If team A wants the penalty, it must be enforced on the try.

PLAY 11: Team B fouls during the last timed down of the fourth period. Team A's score is a (a) touchdown that cuts team B's lead to one point, or (b) field goal that ties the game.

RULING 11: In (a), if team A wants to accept the penalty, it must be assessed on the try. The penalty cannot be enforced on the first play of overtime. In (b), team A may choose a replay of the down or may choose to have the penalty enforced from the succeeding spot (the first play of overtime).

PLAY 12: During the last timed down of the fourth quarter, A1 scores a touchdown to reduce its deficit to one point. During A1's run, B2 is flagged for grasping but not pulling A1's facemask. During the successful kick try, B3 roughs the kicker.

RULING 12: Team A may only have the penalty for the opponent foul on the touchdown-scoring play enforced on the try; it cannot carry over to the overtime. However, team A could choose to have the penalty for B3's roughing on the try enforced from the previous spot with a replay of the down, or choose to have it enforced on the first play of overtime.

If a touchdown is scored during the last timed down of the fourth quarter and there is a foul by the opponent of the scoring team, whether the penalty will be enforced or not depends on the score. If the outcome of the game has been decided and the try is not needed to determine playoff qualification, the penalty is declined and the game is over. However, if the try must be played, the penalty can only be enforced on the try. The try will then be the last play of the game.

PLAY 13: During A1's run for a touchdown during the last timed down of the fourth quarter, his facemask is grasped but not twisted by B1. The touchdown makes the score (a) team A 34, team B 0, (b) team B 21, team A 20, or (c) team B 34, team A 0.

RULING 13: In (a) and (c), if the try is necessary to determine playoff qualification, the penalty may be enforced on the try. If not, the penalty is declined and the game is over. In (b), since team A could tie or win the game with a successful try, team A may choose to have the penalty enforced on the try. The penalty could not bridge to overtime if team A ties the score with a one-point try.

OVERTIME BRIDGES

Some penalties can bridge from one overtime period to the next or bridge from one overtime series to the next. Whenever penalties can bridge from the fourth quarter to overtime, from one overtime series to the next or from one overtime period to the next, it is crucial for the referee to give the offended captain the correct options.

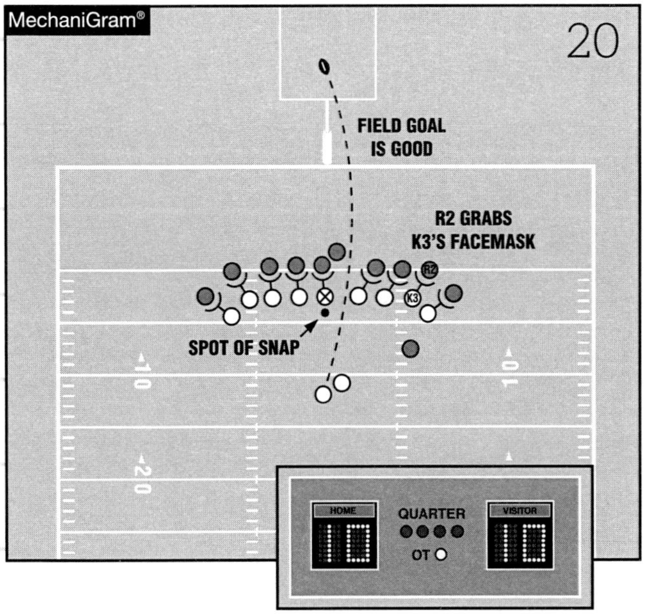

PLAY 14: As seen in MechaniGram 20, in the second series of the first overtime period, K1's successful field goal ties the score. During the play, R2 is flagged for grasping but not twisting K3's facemask.

RULING 14: Team K may choose previous-spot enforcement and replay the down, or have the penalty bridge to the succeeding spot in the next overtime period. In the latter case, if team K begins the overtime on offense, it will snap from team R's five yardline. If team K begins on defense, team R will snap from team K's 15 yardline. In either case it will be first and goal.

PLAY 15: As seen in MechaniGram 21, it is fourth and goal for team K from team R's four yardline in the first series for either team in overtime. K1's successful field goal gives team K a 10-7 lead. During the play, R2 is flagged for roughing the kicker.

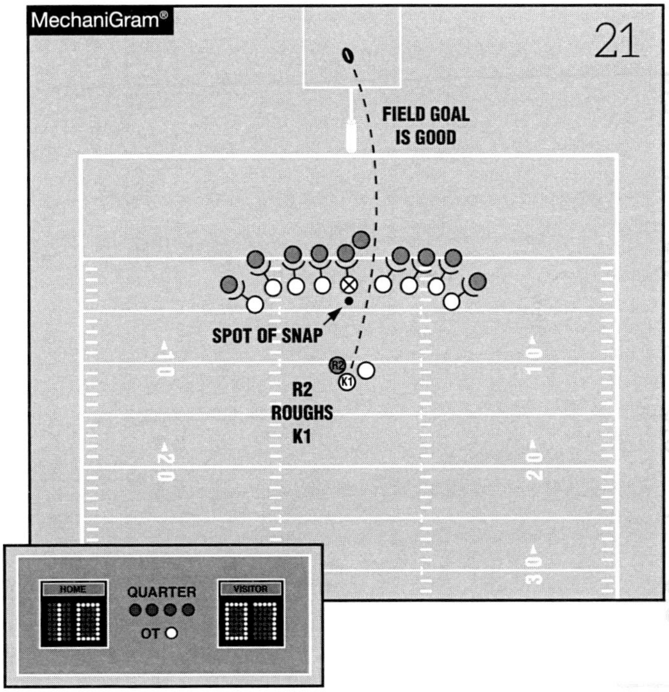

RULING 15: Team K may choose enforcement from the previous spot, yielding first and goal from team B's two yardline, or may choose enforcement from the succeeding spot. That would mean team R would start its overtime series from the opponent's 25 yardline.

PLAY 16: On the second series of the first overtime period, K1's successful field goal or try ties the score. R2 is flagged for (a) cursing the official during the play, or (b) a late hit on K3 after the play.

RULING 16: In (a) and (b), the game will proceed to a second overtime period. If team K wants to accept the penalty, it must be enforced from the succeeding spot. That means if team R starts the second overtime period on offense, it will face first and goal from the opponent's 25 yardline. If team K starts on offense, it will face first and goal from the opponent's five yardline.

PLAY 17: On the second series of the first overtime period, K1's successful field goal or try ties the score. K2 is flagged for (a) cursing the official during the play, or (b) a late hit on R3 after the play.

RULING 17: In (a) and (b), the game will proceed to a second overtime period. If team R wants to accept the penalty, it must be enforced from the succeeding spot. That means if team K starts the second overtime period on offense, it will face first and goal from the opponent's 25 yardline. If team R starts on offense, it will face first and goal from the opponent's five yardline.

PLAY 18: On the second series of the first overtime period, A1's touchdown ties the score. B2 is flagged for (a) cursing the official during the play, or (b) a late hit on A1 after the play.

RULING 18: In (a) or (b), if team A wants to accept the penalty, it must be enforced from the succeeding spot (the try). The penalty cannot bridge to the second overtime period if team A's try fails and the score remains tied.

DEAD-BALL FOUL AFTER A QUARTER

If the penalty is accepted for a dead-ball foul that occurs after time for any period expires, the penalty bridges to the next period or the succeeding spot in overtime.

PLAY 19: After A1 is downed, B2 piles on. The foul occurred after time for the period expired. In (a), the second period expired, in (b) the third period expired, or in (c) the fourth period expired with the score tied.

RULING 19: In (a), the penalty is assessed on the second-half kickoff. In (b) the penalty bridges to the fourth quarter; the third period is not extended. In (c), the penalty bridges to the overtime. Once again, the referee's instructions to the captains must be precise to avoid confusion.

CHAPTER 16

TRIES

TRIES

LIVE-BALL FOUL BY TEAM B ON SUCCESSFUL TRY

↓

TEAM A MAY CHOOSE TO HAVE PENALTY ENFORCED FROM PREVIOUS SPOT AND REPLAY DOWN

OR

TEAM A MAY CHOOSE TO ACCEPT RESULTS OF PLAY AND HAVE PENALTY ENFORCED FROM SUCCEEDING SPOT

TEAM A COMMITS FOUL THAT INCLUDES LOSS OF DOWN

↓

NO REPLAY OF THE DOWN IF THE PENALTY IS ACCEPTED

Note: Live-ball fouls by team B on unsuccessful tries or by team A on successful tries are enforced the same if they occurred during a regular scrimmage play. If team A commits a live-ball foul on an unsuccessful try, team B will likely decline the penalty.

CHAPTER 16

For the most part, fouls on tries are treated the same as fouls that occur on scrimmage plays. Live-ball fouls enforced as dead-ball fouls are always enforced from the succeeding spot and cannot be combined with live-ball fouls to create a double foul.

If team A fouls during an unsuccessful try, there is no replay if team B declines the penalty. There is no bridge to the kickoff or succeeding spot in overtime.

If team A fouls during a successful try, team B must accept the penalty to have the down replayed. The down is over and there is no replay if the foul includes loss of down.

If team B fouls during an unsuccessful try, team A must accept the penalty for team B's foul to get a replay of the down. There is no bridge to the kickoff or succeeding spot in overtime.

If team R fouls during a successful kick try, team K may choose previous-spot enforcement or bridge the penalty to the kickoff or succeeding spot in overtime. If team K accepts the penalty and replays the down, there can be no bridge to the kickoff or extra period. Team R cannot be penalized twice for the same offense.

If team B fouls during a successful two-point try, team A may only choose to bridge the penalty to the kickoff or succeeding spot in overtime. There can be no replay of the down.

The penalty for a foul that occurs during a touchdown-scoring play may bridge to the next kickoff. However, the offended team may still opt for enforcement on the try. Also, the options are different if the scoring play occurs during the last timed down of a quarter (see Chapter 15).

PLAY 1: As seen in MechaniGram 22, K1 is attempting a kick try from team R's three yardline. R2 grasps but does not twist K3's facemask at the line of scrimmage and R4 roughs kicker K1. The kick is successful.

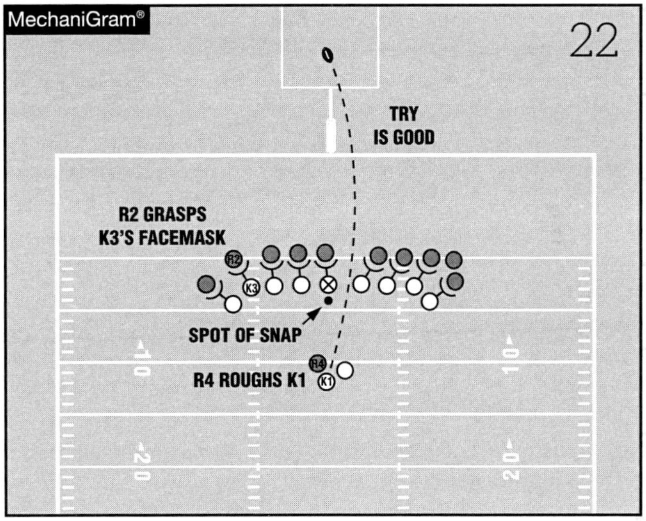

RULING 1: Team K may choose to have one of the penalties enforced from the previous spot and a replay of the down, or choose to have one of the penalties enforced on the kickoff or from the succeeding spot in overtime. Team K does not have the option of accepting previous-spot enforcement for one foul and bridging the other foul to the kickoff or succeeding spot in overtime.

PLAY 2: With 4:37 to play in the first quarter, team A attempts a try from team B's three yardline. B1 grasps but does not twist A2's facemask during A2's run. The try is good for two points.

RULING 2: Since the penalty may bridge to the kickoff, team A will likely choose to accept the penalty with succeeding-spot enforcement.

CHAPTER 16

If during a touchdown-scoring play either team commits a foul that has succeeding-spot enforcement, the penalty may be enforced on either the try or on the next kickoff. The same choice exists for the penalty for a foul that occurs after a touchdown and before the initial ready-for-play signal on the ensuing try. In essence, all fouls that occur by the opponents of the scoring team from the moment the scoring play begins through the ready for play on the try have the same penalty options.

PLAY 3: A1's run from scrimmage results in a touchdown. During A1's run, B1 is flagged for (a) grasping but not twisting A1's facemask, or (b) cursing the official.

RULING 3: In (a) or (b), the touchdown counts and team A may choose to have the penalty enforced on the try or on the subsequent kickoff.

PLAY 4: A1's run from scrimmage results in a touchdown. After the ball has crossed the goalline, (a) B1 tackles A1, or (b) B1 curses the official.

RULING 4: In (a) and (b), the touchdown counts. In (a), because the dead-ball foul occurred before the ready signal for the ensuing try, team A may choose to have the penalty enforced on the try or on the subsequent kickoff. In (b), because an unsportsmanlike foul has succeeding-spot enforcement, team A has the option to choose enforcement on the try or on the next kickoff.

PLAY 5: A1's run from scrimmage results in a touchdown. After A1's run, B1 is flagged for a dead-ball foul. Team A's captain chooses to have the penalty enforced on the subsequent kickoff. During the successful try, team B's coach is flagged for unsportsmanlike conduct.

RULING 5: If team A wants to accept the penalty for unsportsmanlike conduct, it must be enforced on the subsequent kickoff along with the previously accepted foul. That would result in team A kicking off from team B's 30 yardline.

PLAY 6: Team A trails by seven points when A1's run results in a touchdown as time runs out for the second quarter. B2 is flagged for a personal foul (a) during, or (b) after A1's touchdown-scoring run.

RULING 6: In (a) and (b), the touchdown counts. In either case, team A may choose to have the penalty enforced on the try or on the kickoff to start the third quarter.

PLAY 7: Team A trails by seven points when A1's run results in a touchdown as time runs out for the fourth quarter. B2 is flagged for a personal foul (a) during, or (b) after A1's touchdown-scoring run.

RULING 7: In (a) and (b), the touchdown counts. In either case, if team A wants the penalty, it must be enforced on the try. The penalty cannot bridge to overtime if team A ties the score.

PLAY 8: On a try, A1 is flagged for a false start. As the penalty is being enforced, B1 curses the official.

RULING 8: B1's foul occurred after the initial ready-for-play signal (the one that preceded the false start). Team A does not have the option to bridge the penalty to the next kickoff. Dead-ball fouls are enforced in the order in which they occur. Therefore, after the penalty for A1's false start is penalized, the penalty for B1's unsportsmanlike foul is enforced half the distance to the goal. The result is a try from team B's four yardline.

PLAY 9: A1's run from scrimmage results in a touchdown. B1 curses the official (a) before, or (b) after the referee has signaled the ready-for-play for the try.

RULING 9: In (a), team A may choose to have the penalty enforced on either the try or the subsequent kickoff. In (b), because the foul occurred after the ready signal, the penalty must be enforced on the try.

PLAY 10: K1's kick try is good. During the kick, R2 is flagged for roughing K1. After the ball is dead, K3 shoves R2 to the ground.

RULING 10: A live-ball foul by one team and a dead-ball foul by the opponent cannot be paired to create a double foul. Team K may choose to have the penalty for R2's foul enforced from the previous spot or on the subsequent kickoff.

- If team K chooses enforcement from the previous spot, the penalty for K3's foul will be enforced and the try will be repeated from team R's 16-1/2 yardline.
- If team K chooses enforcement on the subsequent kickoff, the penalty is enforced to team R's 45 yardline. The penalty for K3's dead-ball foul

will be enforced from there. Team K would kick off from its own 40 yardline.

When giving team K's captain his options, the referee must be sure to explain that the penalty for his team's foul will be enforced at the same time as the penalty for R2's foul.

CHAPTER 17
SPECIAL ENFORCEMENTS

PlayPic®

SPECIAL ENFORCEMENTS

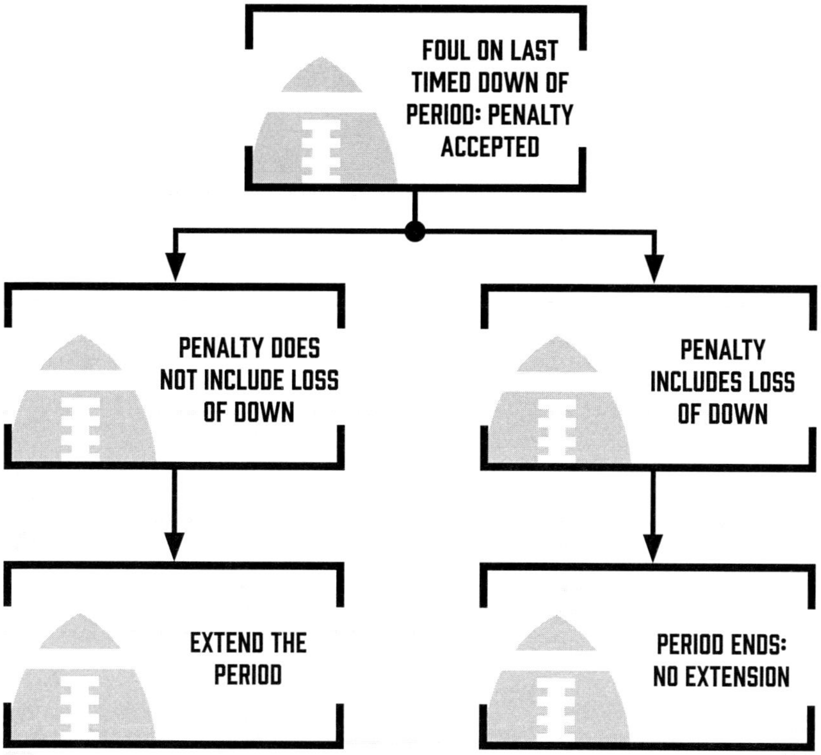

SPECIAL ENFORCEMENTS

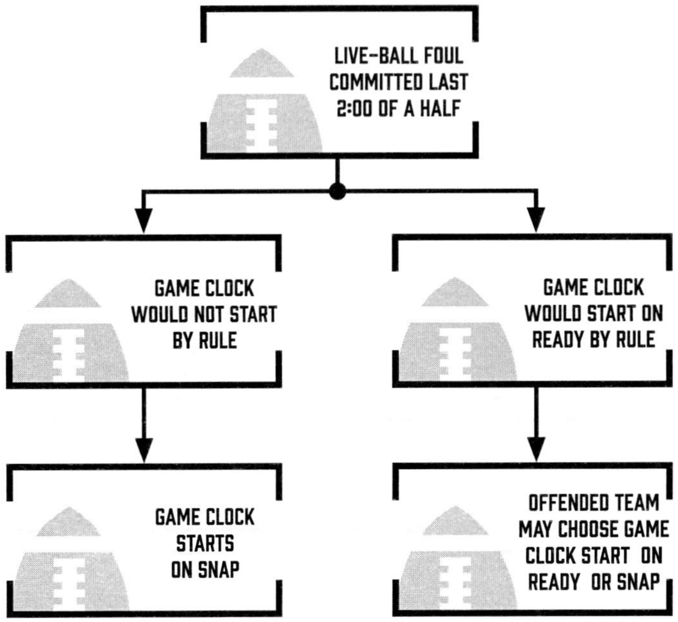

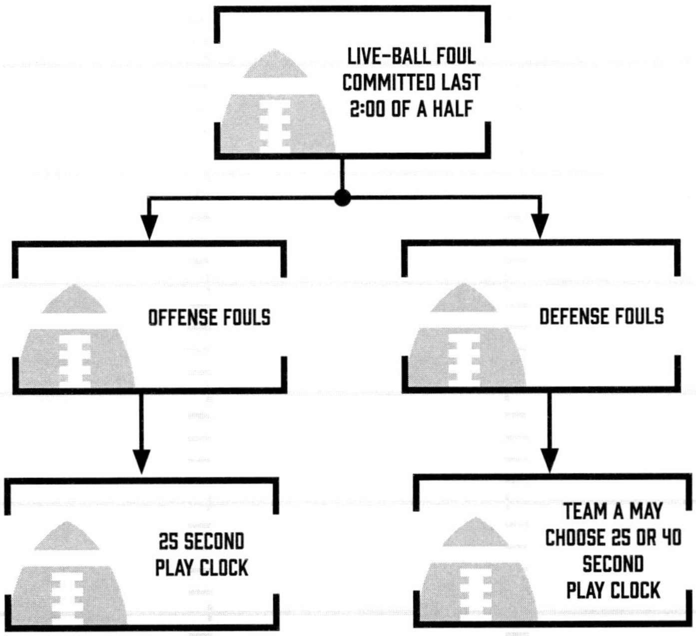

Four fouls result in the award of a new series (automatic first down). Four result in the loss of the right to replay a down (loss of down).

There are circumstances that result in the offended team choosing whether the game clock starts on the ready for play or on the snap and whether the play clock is set at 40 or 25 seconds.

AUTOMATIC FIRST DOWN

The penalties that include an automatic first down are roughing the passer, roughing the kicker, roughing the holder and roughing the snapper.

Roughing the passer is covered in Chapter 7. Penalties for the other roughing fouls are enforced from the previous spot. Remember that if those fouls occur on a scoring play, there is a possibility they may bridge to the next period or the succeeding kickoff (see Chapter 15).

LOSS OF DOWN

Fouls that include loss of down are illegal forward handing, illegal forward pass by team A and intentional grounding.

The loss of down aspect of a penalty has no significance following a change of possession or if the line to gain is reached after enforcement. That coincides with the fundamental that no series may begin on a down other than first.

PLAY 1: Third and three at team A's 27 yardline. A1 runs to team A's 40 yardline, then throws a forward pass to A2. A2 advances to team B's 20 yardline.

CHAPTER 17

RULING 1: An illegal forward pass is enforced as a running play and penalty enforcement is from the spot of the foul. The penalty leaves the ball at team A's 35 yardline, which is beyond the line to gain. Even though the penalty for an illegal forward pass includes a loss of down, team A will have first and 10 from its 35 yardline.

If during a successful try, a loss of down foul by A occurs, there is no score and no replay.

If a foul for which the penalty includes loss of down occurs on the last timed down of a period, the period is not extended.

PLAY 2: Third and three at team A's 27 yardline. A1 runs to team A's 40 yardline, then throws a forward pass to A2, who advances for a touchdown. Time for the second quarter expires during the play.

RULING 2: Team B has to accept the penalty to nullify the touchdown. Because the penalty includes a loss-of-down provision, the period is not extended.

The referee has the authority to start or stop the clock if a team attempts to conserve or consume time illegally at any point in the game.

PLAY 3: With less than two minutes remaining in the second period, there is a false start by A1 clearly for the purpose of stopping the clock.

RULING 3: Team B shall have the option to start the clock on the snap.

GAME/PLAY CLOCK OPTION

When a foul is committed with less than two minutes remaining in either half, the offended team has the option to start the game clock on the snap.

PLAY 4: Team B trails, 14-7, with 1:30 remaining in the game. Third and 10 on team A's 10 yardline. A1's run gains two yards and ends inbounds. A2 is flagged for holding during the run.

RULING 4: Team B may decline the yardage penalty by having the clock start on the snap.

PLAY 5: Team A trails, 14-7, with 1:30 remaining in the game. Third and 10 on team A's own 10 yardline. A1's pass to A2 gains 35 yards and the play ends inbounds. B2 is flagged for pass interference.

RULING 5: Team A will decline the penalty for the interference foul,. Team A will choose to have the game clock start on the snap.

With less than two minutes remaining in either half, the offense may choose a 40-second play clock when the defense is the only team to commit a foul.

PLAY 6: Team A leads, 14-7, with 1:30 remaining in the game and the game clock running. Third and 10 on team A's 10 yardline. Team B is flagged for encroachment.

RULING 6: Team A will accept the penalty. Because the play clock will be set to 40 seconds and the game clock will start on the ready signal, team B gains no time advantage by fouling.

CHAPTER 17

PLAY 7: Team A trails, 14-7, with 1:30 remaining in the game and the game clock running. Third and 10 on team A's 10 yardline. A1's pass to A2 gains 35 yards and the play ends inbounds. B2 is flagged for pass interference.

RULING 7: Team A will decline the penalty for the interference foul, yielding first and 10 from its own 45 yardline. The play clock will be set to 40 seconds and team A will choose to have the game clock start on the snap.

If both teams commit live-ball fouls, the penalties cancel, the game clock starts by rule and the play clock is set to 25 seconds.

PLAY 8: Team A leads, 14-7, with 1:30 remaining in the game and the game clock running. Third and 10 on team A's 10 yardline. A1's pass to A2 gains 35 yards and the play ends inbounds. B2 is flagged for pass interference and A3 is flagged for holding.

RULING 8: The fouls offset and the down is replayed. The play clock is set to 25 seconds and the game clock starts on the ready signal.

PENALTY SUMMARY

LOSS OF 5 YARDS	SIGNAL
Delay of game	7-21
Illegal substitution	22
Free-kick infraction	7-19
Encroachment	7-18
Free kick out of bounds	19
Invalid or illegal fair-catch signal	32
Snap infraction	7-19
False start	7-19
Illegal formation	19
Less than seven players on team A's line or numbering violation	19
Illegal shift or illegal motion	20
Planned loose-ball infraction	19
Illegally handing ball forward (also loss of down)	35-9
Illegal forward pass (by team A) (also loss of down)	35-9
Illegal forward pass (by team B)	35
Intentional grounding (also loss of down)	36-9
Ineligible receiver illegally downfield	37
Illegal touching (also loss of down)	16-9
Helping runner	44
Incidental grasping of opponent's facemask, or any helmet opening, chin strap or attached tooth and mouth protector	45
Running into kicker/holder	30
Sideline interference	7-29
Attendant illegally on field	19
Nonplayer outside of the team box, but not on field	7-29

LOSS OF 10 YARDS

	SIGNAL
Illegal blocking technique	42
Interlocked blocking	44
Holding	42
Runner grasping a teammate	42
Illegal use of hands or arms	42
Illegal block in the back	43
Illegal block on free kicks	43
Illegally kicking or batting ball	31

LOSS OF 15 YARDS

	SIGNAL
Unsportsmanlike conduct by player or nonplayer	24
Illegal helmet contact against a defenseless player	24
Illegal block after valid or invalid fair-catch signal	43
Illegal blindside block	38-26
Kick-catching interference	33
Forward-pass interference	33
If intentional an additional 15 yards	27
Illegal block below waist or on free-kicker or holder	40
Clipping	39
Chop block	41
Tripping	46
Illegal personal contact outside restricted area	38
Charging into an opponent obviously out of the play	38
Grasping an opponent's facemask or any helmet opening, chin strap or attached tooth and mouth protector	38-45
Butt block, face tackle or spear (illegal helmet contact)	24
Horse-collar tackle	38-25
Initiate contact with helmet-less opponent	38
Targeting an opponent	38-24

PENALTY SUMMARY CONTINUED

Roughing passer (also first down)	34
Roughing kicker or holder (also first down)	38-30
Roughing snapper (also first down)	38
Slapping blocker's head	38
Illegal personal contact in restricted area	38-29
Illegal participation	28
Participating without a helmet beyond immediate action	28
Sideline interference (third and subsequent)	7-29-27
Nonplayer illegally on field	27
Unfair acts	27

DISQUALIFICATION ASSOCIATED WITH CERTAIN 15-YARD PENALTIES	SIGNAL
Fighting by player or nonplayer	38-47
Intentionally contacting an official	38-47
Striking, kicking, kneeing	38-47
Any act if unduly rough or flagrant (give proper signal and follow with 47)	47
A second unsportsmanlike foul by player or nonplayer	27-47
A substitute leaving team box during a fight	27-47

SIGNAL CHART

Ready for play
* Untimed down

Start the clock

Stop the clock

TV/radio timeout

Touchdown/field goal/
point(s) after touchdown

Safety

Dead-ball foul,
touchback
(arm waved side to side)

SIGNAL CHART CONTINUED

First down

Loss of down

Incomplete pass/ unsuccessful try or field goal/penalty declination/ coin toss option deferred

Legal touching

Inadvertent whistle

Disregard flag

End of period

Sideline warning

First touching
Illegal touching

Encroachment
NOTE: Signal 17 is not depicted because it is an NCAA-only signal.

False start
Illegal formation
Free kick infraction

Illegal motion (1 hand)
Illegal shift (2 hands)

Delay of game

Substitution infraction

Equipment violation

Illegal helmet contact
Targeting

Illegal horse-collar

SIGNAL CHART CONTINUED

Illegal blindside block

Unsportsmanlike conduct or noncontact foul

Illegal participation

Sideline interference
Note: face press box

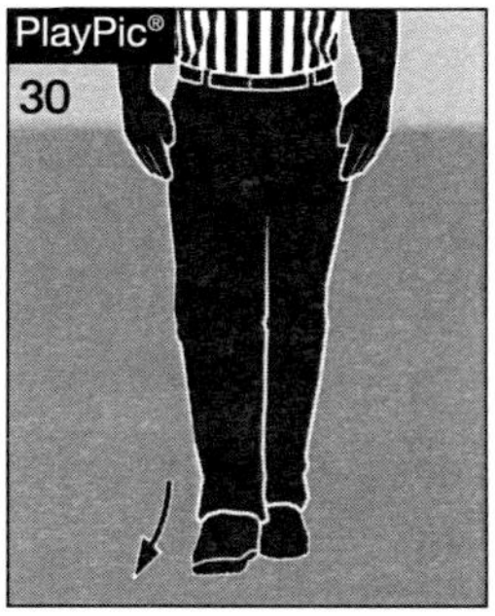

Running into or roughing the kicker or holder

Illegal batting/kicking
(for illegal kicking, follow with point toward foot)

Illegal/invalid fair catch

Pass interference
Kick-catching interference

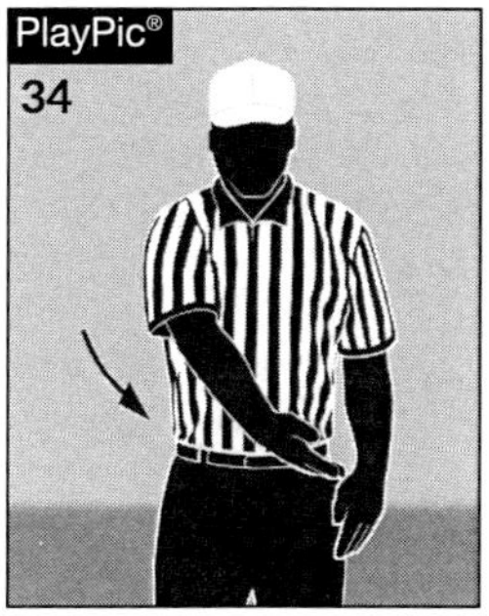

Roughing the passer

Illegal pass
Illegal forward handing
Note: face press box

Intentional grounding

Ineligible downfield
on pass

Personal foul

Clipping

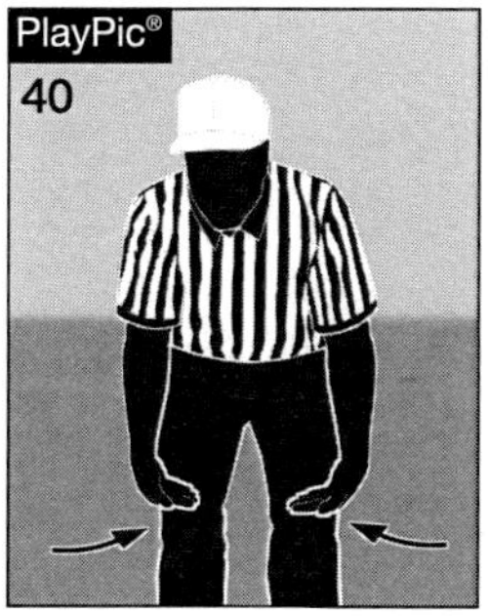

Block below the waist
Illegal block

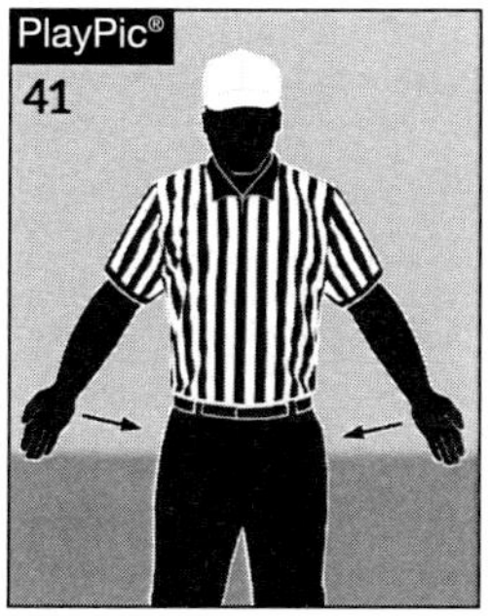

Chop block

Holding
Illegal use of
hands or arms

SIGNAL CHART CONTINUED

Illegal block in the back

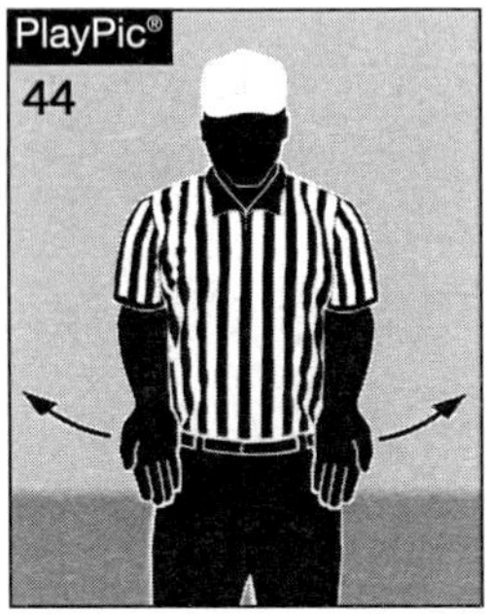

Helping the runner
Interlocked blocking

Grasping of facemask,
helmet opening or
chin strap

Tripping

Disqualification